Self-E

3 Manuscripts in 1 Book, Including: Assertiveness,
Social Skills and Persuasion

Lawrence Finnegan

More by Lawrence Finnegan

Discover all books from the Communication Skills Series by Lawrence Finnegan at:

bit.ly/lawrence-finnegan

Book 1: Body Language

Book 2: Assertiveness

Book 3: Conversation Skills

Book 4: Persuasion

Book 5: Make People Laugh

Book 6: Small Talk

Book 7: Social Skills

Book 8: Email Etiquette

Themed book bundles available at discounted prices:

bit.ly/lawrence-finnegan

Copyright

Table of Contents

Book 1: Assertiveness

7 Easy Steps to Master Assertive Social Confidence, Self-Esteem, Self-Awareness & Social Dynamics

Lawrence Finnegan

Introduction

Welcome to "Assertiveness". This guide is for people at all skill levels in this ability, whether you are a shrinking violet who can barely speak up in group settings or a sharp-talking hotshot already in command of social situations. There are tips you have not tried, aspects of interpersonal communication you have not considered, and lessons to learn. Operating under the assumption that you want to learn how to persuade and convince at most or inspire and motivate at least, we break down exactly what it takes to be assertive in the Information Age.

We will go through seven easy exercises you can practice to be more assertive. The career advancement and personal enrichment gained by asserting yourself more is almost beside the point: baseline mental health. Far from being reserved for influential leaders or exploited by arrogant people, assertiveness is necessary for a healthy and balanced personality. Because at the very *least*, you need a tiny bit to feel safe, confident, and comfortable even in small groups.

Using a little biology and psychology as we go along, I use science and research wherever possible to back up these techniques with facts. You won't have to take my word for anything, nor should you: a large part of asserting yourself efficiently is credibility. Gone are the days we wave our hand at a persuasive individual and say they "just have charisma." It is nothing special; no inherent knack someone is born with. We now know *precisely* what a compelling, influential person does to shine. Our understanding of the human mind and universal social drives allow us to assert our will with force *and* grace.

Self-esteem, self-worth, and getting anywhere in life demand you assert your will at least a little. Often, the prize goes not to the best or the brightest but to the one who spoke up and stepped forward. Stop letting the extroverted or opinionated lead by default and no more allowing someone with more social confidence to call the shots simply because no one else did. Learn how to lead the conversation without taking all the air out of it.

Master the art of facilitating, not issuing orders, by simple actions and basic behaviors in any group. Defuse hotheads, coax activity from the reticent and, at the very least, make sure you are not ignored. Wolf packs in the wild are led by an equal mated pair, the myth of the Alpha Wolf a construct of narcissism and arrogance. Be the invisible leader, guiding others toward objectives you offered or a radiant beacon, leading the way through example and trust.

There is quite simply no aspect of life not improved by learning how to exert your will in a meaningful and polite manner. So, take a few moments to consider your place in social situations as we take a deep dive into the complex and nuanced world of assertiveness.

Let's get started!

Chapter 1: Step 1 - Healthy Boundaries

Asserting yourself has one key component that we must consider as we make our way through this project. First and foremost, a firm accounting of our personal boundaries protects against manipulation by others and us accidentally manipulating people. A blanket term for our personal space, belief system and emotional needs, establishing and maintaining healthy boundaries also ensures a solid work/life balance and we are not burning ourselves out. We have to place limits on our give and take, or we wind up exhausted at best or taken advantage of at worst.

Boundaries

Individuals have the obvious physical boundaries, our sense of personal space and how much of that space we want to share with another. We have mental barriers, emotional and intellectual, which we develop to make sure we are not jerked around or manipulated. Sexual desires and varying levels of intimacy help us pair-bond and we draw distinct and important boundaries around our love lives. Many of us have religious or spiritual boundaries, an ethos or philosophy we use to inspire and guide us. If you lack monetary and material boundaries, then you are either independently wealthy or chronically cash strapped. We can place limitations on our time, romantic interests and anything, really, as long we express these limits early and often.

We have the right to assert our needs without feeling bad about it. It should go without saying that this needs to be done in a respectful way. You can ask for the moon as long as you do so with a smile and expectation that it will be refused; you are ready to handle a No with good cheer but still asked! They know your intent. Should the moon become available, they will know you are interested.

Assertiveness and aggression not the same things.

Neither are assertiveness and persuasion. While there is plenty of overlap between asserting yourself and persuading someone else, there is virtually no point where you have to resort to aggression. If putting up or maintaining boundaries if difficult for you, this lesson is one of learning how to stand up for yourself, if less exerting your will. If you have too many walls in place already, this lesson is one in tearing down and letting in. As ever, there is a fine balance to be achieved in maintaining a social equilibrium between "going with the flow" and "sticking to your guns".

In our personal lives, ill-defined or undefended boundaries can look like friends coming over unannounced- if you don't like that; some people enjoy unexpected guests! It can look like someone over extended and exhausted because they never learned to say No *or* lazy and unfulfilled because they never learned to say Yes. We can do an awful lot toward ensuring these crucial personal defenses are strong if we start early.

Know Core, Know Boundaries

1. Set them early
2. Set them consistently
3. Reflect on them
4. Feel free to reset them
5. Talk about them
6. Know your deal breakers; non-negotiable

As long as your boundaries are already established when you meet someone, this one takes care of itself. Reflection is number three, but if we go into a situation with boundaries in place, we can save ourselves and those around us the awkward and uncomfortable situation of having to change our expectations of interpersonal behavior after the fact. That can be damaging to a relationship, professional or otherwise, so setting standards first thing is crucial. So, make sure you consider what might be asked of you before going into any situation, so someone who knows exactly what they are after doesn't hustle you toward their own end before you have had a chance to consider.

Consistency is key, not being huggy and intimate one day then uncaring and apathetic the next.

Guard against retreating into your clique at work or school completely. Us Vs. Them, tribal thinking is the detriment of any larger social group and the more we can identify our similarities and act on them, instead of our differences, the better. Consistent enforcement of boundaries is important, so others know what to expect from us, giving people a chance to learn our needs.

Reflection is going to make sure your behavior stays updated. The last decade, 2010s, has seen social changes the likes of which we haven't seen since the 1960s. Taking time to think about your actions in the world and how they affect the corners of society you touch makes sure you don't fall behind. On the other hand, reflecting on the past and how we got to where we are is also important. One part philosophy and one part autobiography, thinking about your day and especially your interactions will give you insight into what level of assertion you need to work on.

Feel free to move your boundaries. In fact, they *have* to move. These are psychological constructs, not literal barriers. If you form these too solidly you risk stodgy, rigidity. It is good to have strong willpower, but only up to the point it serves you. Once that idea you are clinging to no longer helps you grow, makes you happy or otherwise works positively in your life it is time to break those constraints and reform them elsewhere. A lot of folks are perfectly happy breaking boundaries but then forget to establish new ones, or allow the new limit to be placed in an unhealthy position.

Reflect on yourself, but do not get lost in a maze of mirrors. Too much self-referential introspection can very easily lead you to wrong conclusions. Talk to others, or risk running around in a personal consensus circle. Talking to others, about ideas and concepts not things and people, is vital to personal development in general, setting and resetting our personal boundaries in particular.

Honestly, even if we find ourselves lacking in a trusted person to use as a sounding board, the act of externalizing our thoughts and feelings can be strong, to. Journalism, word clouds, collage and any kind of thought mapping is OK but in reality that's another facet of reflection. A real human with their own boundaries, hopefully similar to ours, is often the only way to get a solid impression of how our interactions (and no actions!) are going over.

No Core, No Boundaries

Finally, much is made of flexibility and adaptability, of being able to go with the flow, that it can be easy to forget to mention that you are allowed to have some non-negotiables. For emphasis: you NEED a few deal-breakers to anchor you in place, to offer stillness in an otherwise endlessly churning world. The adage "If you don't stand for something, you'll fall for anything" comes to mind. The search for personal axioms (an Axiom is technically an unchanging rule which applies universally but let's limit it to your own personal space) is an interesting one; there are very few rules which apply at all times under all circumstances.

Usually, you have a pretty good idea about what you quite simply will not tolerate, cannot stand and will not abide. All too often, we find ourselves bound up in hard and fast rules which limit us, stunt our growth and keep our horizons narrow. Few of us need to learn to set limits, "nail a toe to the floor" as the saying goes, or otherwise form at least one personal law. More often than not we need to work on tearing down the wall, freeing ourselves up to be more flexible.

The more we reconsider, accommodate and bend, the more room we make for growth. Not all change is good change, which is why reflection and talking to others is so important. However, if our initial roots aren't sunk into something hard, we risk getting blown away. Unpacking that metaphor is knowing what you have decided is going to be unchanging is worth sinking your foundation into. Religions fill this role most often, however the modern age has proven those institutions to be just as fallible as any, and more than one spiritual edifice has demonstrated it would rather circle the wagons and defend the hierarchy then open up its halls and expel the wrong doers in its ranks.

Self-Control

Real steadfast personalities do what is right in all circumstances but the very best of humanity also does the right thing when no one is watching. It is easy to do the right thing when there are eyes on you, but how do you behave when left to your own devices? Asserting yourself can be hardest of all when it is simply Me, Myself and I.

In the dark of night, or those hours when we have no one but ourselves to hold us accountable, can be the most difficult. Drinking, smoking, all manner of personal vices can seem like such personal demons it seems irrelevant to a conversation about interpersonal communication. But the fight for enough self-possession to assert ourselves in society begins with the self and your ability to stand up for yourself, to maintain your personal boundaries no matter the countervailing sentiment against, will be immeasurably easier when you have the discipline and fortitude to practice what you preach.

Chapter 2: Step 2 - Confidence

Confidence is *not* to be confused with being pushy, overly opinionated, or rude.

When I say "confident," what do you imagine? Most people will picture a male with their chest puffed out, chin up, and shoulders back, smiling, usually with balled fists and a long stride. I challenge that entire notion, deconstruct what 'confidence' is and how it is projected, letting you decide what type you wish to exude.

Exude means to generate something subtly, so effortlessly that nobody is sure where it came from. Because as we work on being *more* confident, we always have to be on the lookout for over-compensating, being pushy, or militant. Your confidence should be the carrier, not the message. Ambition is only inspiring up to a point; beyond that point, you must rely on not only being right but expressing yourself in a way that doesn't intimidate others.

#1 in confidence training: you HAVE to "fake it 'til you make it". If you feel unsure, insecurity will creep into every thought and action until that diffidence robs you of all credibility. Like anything, Practice Makes Perfect, and even something that feels like an essential part of our demeanor you can condition toward change.

1. Preparation
2. Make eye contact
3. Speak up!
4. Articulate; no filler words
5. Animate: gesture, emote and move around

Preparing

Not rushing in blind, not relying 100% on improvisation, and generally getting ahead of things is so crucial I give it a whole chapter all to itself further on. As it relates to confidence, there can be no doubt if you prepare for something, you'll feel better about it. It is impossible to plan for every eventuality, so this might even be the illusion of preparedness. It's been said that no battle plan ever survived its first encounter with an enemy because, so often, life throws us curveballs. Whether or not we can deal with those unexpected challenges will depend mainly on what we did to get ready.

In paratrooper school, they spend the first week teaching you how to fall. Such is life, the adage Plan For the Worst But Expect the Best comes to mind. You can rehearse and practice all you want (and you should!), but you should always expect the unexpected. Practice laughing off surprises, meeting challenges with a smile, and not letting your emotions carry you away. You can remain cool when things get heated, having imagined worst-case scenarios or basic flubs and how you would deal with them.

Thoughts can trigger the brain's emotional responses almost as easily as experiences, so you can use guided imagery to go through things before you ever have to live them. If practical, hands-on practice is impossible, consciously go through a situation in your mind, walk through it step by step, realistically. Imagine doing it perfectly. You must be thinking of things that can and have happened. You want to use memory more than imagination as much as possible, so you have to be thinking of plausible things, things you have done before if you can. This way, once you are up and doing it for the first time, a part of your brain has already done it.

Eye Contact

This one is so crucial, dare I say integral, to projecting confidence and assertiveness in general. If you have a hard time making and maintaining eye contact, you can use all sorts of tricks and workaround to fake it until you get over it. You *have* to address this issue if you are guilty of a downcast gaze, darting eyes, or not looking at who's speaking or listening. Eye contact is a vital component of active listening and speaking, as you appear confident in either case.

However, nobody wants you *drilling a hole in their head*, either. What a colorful expression we have for staring at someone too hard, but it is apt: it can feel deeply unsettling when someone is using too much eye contact. "She was staring daggers at me" and "if looks could kill" are all typical cliches that emphasize the weight of your gaze, as well. The other side of the coin has terms like "shrinking violet," "wall-flower," and "bump on a log." All the sayings related to people not being confident, of not making eye contact, are vegetables! While synonyms for confidence are decidedly animalistic: Fierce, Ambitious, and Forceful.

At the beginning of a conversation, make sure you greet the person or group with a smile and a bit of prolonged eye contact. When you deliver a greeting, you want the recipient to feel warm, welcome, and even important. Check in during the conversation by looking at them occasionally, or with glances at least. Again, you don't want to stare deeply into their eyes the entire time. Neither do you want to be staring off into space, down or up, either. In the end, another span of longer than usual eye contact will seal the conversation and make the other person feel special.

If you are having difficulty meeting people's eyes, you can cheat a little bit by glancing at the bridge of their nose, the temple, or areas *near* the eyes. You have to be careful with this tip because we are hardwired, from a biological standpoint, to track where people are looking. In a group, this cheat is easier; you can readily fake out eye contact at a distance, too. In the end, use repetition and practice to master effective eye contact. It's too important to ignore or rely on tricks alone.

Speak Up!

No mumbling, looking down while you speak, or soft voices allowed. You will project, enunciate, and, if you make a presentation before even a small group, you will speak at a slightly slower pace than is natural. Projecting is not shouting. It is putting just a little wind in your words, though, and adding a bit more air between words (if needed). The larger the audience, the more of a pause you might want to consider adding between words. A slightly slower speaking voice not only gives echo's a chance to die down but gives the audience a chance to think about your words.

Overdo it, and you sound slow, maybe even dull. The speed at which you talk is relatively unconscious, and you should take care when trying to relearn a tempo in which to speak. Since talking faster is rarely required (or even possible), it is usually a matter of remembering to slow down if you are a fast-talker or nervous, rather than learning to pick up the pace.

Articulation

Good pronunciation is another excellent reason to study and practice first. Know the words you are going to use. Pronounce the multi-syllabic ones clearly, but don't hurry through smaller words, either. One of the biggest challenges of any public speaker is removing "uh," "ah," and other filler words from a presentation. In casual conversation, those types of sounds can be OK. Still, any time you formally address a group, talk to impress, or are otherwise trying to demonstrate confidence, not peppering your conversation with those non-words will benefit you.

The famous 'water sip' is a great way to stop mid-sentence. Besides even a short talk drying your mouth, pausing to sip water gives the speaker a moment to think. If the topic is complex or emotionally charged, halting and even restarting mid-sentence will be persuasive, demonstrating that you care enough to choose words carefully. In general, just reminding yourself to slow down a little will give you all the time you need to think about what you are saying, speak each word clearly and confidently while giving your listener a chance to consider what you say.

Animated

Body language can be challenging to learn, if only because changing how we naturally move about the world requires getting into between some pretty foundational behaviors. Body language also cuts deeply into culture and upbringing. Some parts of the world are known for their animated body language; some are reserved and subdued. Well, time to reconsider your place in the world!

When you are on stage, and the bigger the stage, the more this is true, the broader, elaborate, and even exaggerated gestures and movements you should make. It's a rule on television that you arrange the characters closer than expected, and the opposite is true in stagecraft. When many people are viewing you, go BIG! Gesture broadly, smile, grimace and frown like you're talking to a child. It is *almost* impossible to overdo this lesson. In its over-application, your message gets lost in the delivery as your antics overshadow what you are saying. But you'll almost always pull yourself back before it comes to that, and audiences love an animated presenter.

Stride back and forth on any stage, but make sure it is in a bid to address the entire crowd; convey confidence and try to meet everyone's eye. If there's a podium or an expectation of a more reserved delivery, then it's all in the arms and head. Your face should convey the emotional tenor of your words, and if you are more stoic, it might be a good idea to practice facial mobility. Mirrors and selfie videos can be a good tool if you lack a willing test audience.

Balance

A fine line exists between Confident and Militant. Sometimes the delineation between the two is personal; one employee thinks the boss is a heavy-handed tyrant, the other find their leadership style firm but fair. Honing your delivery to be persuasive and subtle, guide rather than direct is to know real compelling power. People automatically follow a confident leader but stubbornly resist when they feel they are controlled arbitrarily. However, once a person is confident in you, it is almost frightening how much of your will you can assert over them.

History is full of people using their powers of assertiveness in terrible ways. The right kind of confidence is contagious, and the charmer leads others toward actions they regret almost as soon as you remove the charismatic leader. That's why it's crucial to learn how to lead with quiet confidence, exerting your will by suggestion and open-ended questions. It is not always possible or desirable to dictate and command. Let people come to your conclusions on their own, and there's no need to assert any further.

Chapter 3: Step 3 - Prepare

We glanced at this earlier, but we have to drill down into the topic when you consider how much impact a knowledgeable, practiced speaker can make.

Rehearse, practice or test, at *least* once! Research and practice your topic beforehand, as much as you can. Developing and researching, test runs and study, will go a long way toward giving you the authority and bearing you need.

Research

Studying should not be dull or dry, because you will not retain the information as well, so always look for an approach to a new subject you enjoy, if the topic itself is boring. Suppose you do not like reading, then you can usually find videos or audiobooks that cover what you need to learn. Not only will investigating your topic give you the confidence to tackle any questions your audience might have, but the extra knowledge you possess will be noticeable, even without answering direct inquiries from the listener.

Your tone of voice, body language, and word choice all change when you have a firm understanding of your subject matter. Use this subtle edge to your advantage by becoming an expert on whatever subject you need to discuss confidently. Even if the person doesn't respect your facts, the self-possession and even aplomb you bring to the table will be persuasive all on its own. At first, you can fake this confidence, sure, but sometimes you might have to present something on the fly. However, in most cases, you will have time to familiarize yourself with something at least, if not become an expert on the subject.

Rehearse

Always practice speeches and presentations beforehand, if only just once, but the more times you can run through something you need to present, the better. Write it all out, or at least give yourself some talking points and do a Dry Run. If you lack a co-worker or someone to provide you with feedback, record yourself. Seeing it yourself can be jarring, and if you are the type of person to be overly critical of yourself, this step might make it worse.

Getting over that kind of crippling self-deprecation is crucial to asserting yourself, and it is past time you began pushing through that fear.

No matter how you do a run-through, practice is crucial. Even if you cannot practice for real, take the time to imagine yourself doing whatever it is. The power of positive visualizations is tricking your brain into thinking you have done something before, so make sure and be as realistic as possible when you imagine yourself confidently holding forth. Go through the motions, picture it all as clearly and realistically as you can. As I said in the Confidence chapter earlier on, there are pretty significant sections of your brain that cannot distinguish between what we have thought of and what we have done. Take advantage of this biological hard-wiring instead of being a victim to it.

There is another excellent reason to make recordings and review them, and it's the very sound of your voice. Sure, you are going to perfect the particular occasion you practice for, but do this enough times, over a long enough period, and you will improve the overall quality of your speaking voice, too. Everyone is surprised when they hear themselves played back the first time. "Oh my gosh, do I sound like that?" is a common exclamation. This is because we are used to feeling the vibration of our voices through our inner ear, so we always sound a lot more resonant to ourselves. Once we begin recording, listening, and making changes, we like what we hear better. Eventually, the tenor and pitch of your regular speaking voice get into the act, and you sound more and more confident.

Audience Knowledge

Knowing who you are talking to is an essential part of prep work, as well. Are you addressing a group of peers or a room of mixed age and backgrounds? Someone coming to the wrong group with a speech prepared for another is hilarious in a comedy but will turn into drama really quick if it happens to you. "Know your audience" means talking to a crowd like individuals in a group. Touring acts greet the city by name; motivational speakers at a job site will start name-dropping the boss or local lunch spot; you should find a little something to mention when talking as an outsider to an in-group. Be careful, though, as nothing will chill your reception like mishandling a local favorite.

For the most part, not much should change if the audience does. Your confidence is borne of research and tested in practice. In a professional or public setting, you should not be inserting a bunch of off-topic or anecdotal information anyway, so whatever you have researched and rehearsed should be enjoyable to anyone.

However, your introductory "ice-breaker" comments might change: jokes, local topics, and current events are so inconsistent if you do find yourself presenting material prepared for one group to another, make sure to update any of those kinds of elements. Even if you miss something and accidentally say something which makes it obvious your address was intended for another group, you can usually laugh it off or otherwise spin it in a positive direction. Because misspeaking and public embarrassment is a universal human experience, audiences are very forgiving.

Tailoring your content to your target demographic will always be rewarding, however, so don't diffuse a pointed message by trying to make it too universal.

We love feeling included. Flattery will get you *everywhere,* but nobody likes an apple polisher. If you find yourself in a position to talk to a group sharing a task or ideology, use in-jokes. Make references only, and I mean *only* the assembled will understand. Cater to humanity's undying need to feel included by including the listener in your presentation; the more intimate the conversation, the more this is true. In one-on-one situations, you mention things the person has said, use their name if you've just met, and talk about the person's interests; if you find yourself talking about yourself too long, call yourself out and give them the old "Well, enough about me...."

Glad-handing the audience and catering to the needs of those around you, like everything, can be taken too far.

At school, work, or recreation, watching someone simper and curry favor with a person they respect is painful to watch. Sucking up, boot licking, brown-nosing; none of the expressions for this behavior are kind. You can cater to an individual a little bit without sounding like an empty-headed Yes Man, though. We all want a friend, but few of us want a toady. In the one-on-one type of exchange, this means not agreeing just to be agreeable, stating opinions, and holding to them even when challenged and otherwise holding your own. In our intimate relationships, this give-and-take a delicate dance: assertiveness and being a jerk changeable sometimes from minute to minute.

To Be or Not to Be

Navigating a persuasive middle ground between certainty and changeability can be tricky. Knowing when to stick to your guns and when to go which way the wind blows is an ever-changing dynamic that you must make on a case-by-case basis. Influential leaders know when to be led, and even the most agreeable partner is there to put their foot down sometimes. Steven Jobs, who turned Apple from a sleepy personal computing company to an international powerhouse, wound up dying because nobody close to him could convince the man to treat his cancer with chemo. He just *knew* a juice diet would do the trick. Having long since chased anyone who might disagree away, he died of a highly treatable form of pancreatic cancer. Never believe your own hype; no one is right all the time.

Look for signs, subtle and obvious, as to how forceful a delivery you should make. As valid for an auditorium full of random people as it is an intimate dinner for two, the amount of pressure you should exert in any situation can change instantly. Being able to adjust tack, make adroit corrections or explanations, and otherwise being able to think on your feet come from practice and confidence.

As much as you have to flex and bend, you must be able to hold your own when what you are saying is counter to the prevailing sentiment. While you want to appeal to the group, you cannot let the group run away with you. We are talking about assertiveness here, not socializing. Even in a casual setting among friends, however, your assertiveness training will come into play. For instance: Charcoal BBQs take at least an hour to heat up, and cooking over a grill takes more time than a conventional oven. Meats grill faster than vegetables. The thicker something is, the longer it will take to cook (but don't scorch it!). Fish cooks up more quickly than most meat. If someone isn't out there wrangling all those things, nobody eats until the party is over, the food gets burned, or something gets left out. Only the most overbearing and unpleasant grill master is ever thought poorly of for this attitude- as long as the food is good!

Staying on task is another element of understanding assertiveness, and we take a closer look at it right now.

Chapter 4: Step 4 - Stay on Task

When learning to assert yourself, your emotions give you passion, but your brain will focus that heat. Fiery emotions can inspire others but can also derail your train of thought or, at worst, rob you of credibility. When we are persuasive, or even just holding firm when someone is trying to change our mind, we must stay in control. In control of ourselves, for sure, but control of the thread of conversation, too. Don't get sidetracked and keep emotions in check. While it is always good to stay in touch with your feelings, you cannot let them rule the day. Emotions are dumb, which is to say emotions are the feeling part of your mind but not the thinking part. Ignore your emotional state at your peril, but be sure to parse your feelings against why you feel it.

Emotional Intelligence

Popular as a buzzword in the 90s, this is simply the ability to navigate the stormy seas of your inner life, getting the most out of your emotions by ignoring those based on your lower self and taking heed when our better side sends a strong signal our way. Hew too closely to your heart, and you are called overly emotional, too sensitive, and weak-willed. Seal your emotions away behind a stony facade, however, and suddenly you are Dictatorial or an Ice Queen, remote, demanding, and unfeeling.

While empathy and understanding will take you far, they won't get you to your destination. We are on the lookout for the emotional state of ourselves and others because we need to know what motivations and desires drive people. That which inspires us is often an emotion, not an idea. But even logic-driven folks use our feelings on a matter to guide our ideals as an aid to navigation; you orient a map to the north even if you will never reach the pole. Understand another person's emotions on a matter, and you can find the pivot point of changing their mind. The ultimate reason to pursue emotional intelligence is to base assertions on facts and not your feelings.

Practice looking for the root of your emotions, back-tracing thoughts to their origin, and getting in touch with why you feel the way you do. Journaling, meditation, and therapy can all help you get to the bottom of what drives you. After all, if you don't know why you do the things you do, how will you ever get others to?

The Information Age has been a double-edged sword as far as science and logic are concerned. Almost all of humanity's information is at our fingertips, right alongside false, misleading, and even dangerous misinformation. Vast swaths of the population have abandoned corroborated, demonstrative reality for what they feel, for what they want to be true.

Control

Maintaining a grip on your feelings is crucial, allowing us time to decide of an emotional reaction is worthy of expression or not. Control is key to staying on task because no one will distract you or change the subject by appealing to your emotions. Control gives you what you need to keep a conversation going in the direction it needs to.

Practice not blurting out the first thing that comes to mind, or practice doing exactly that if you are not assertive enough. The best balance between the two is analyzing your responses *just* enough to ensure it is in keeping with what you are trying to accomplish. Whether it's halting the spread of a strong reaction so you can remain articulate or talking to someone who doesn't respect a strong emotional response, knowing how to screw the lid on excitement is all part of operating in the adult world. As much as we try to honor emotions in this era, please don't take it too far.

When you are sure that asserting yourself is what you want and the situation needs, usually the softer your touch, the better. There is a French term, *eminence grise*, translating to Gray Eminence. It refers to a powerful decision-maker or advisor who operates behind the official ruler, influencing and controlling from a subtle remove. While this example is usually hyperbole, it is wholly possible to lead a horse to water *and* make them drink as long as you can convince them they are thirsty. Real power is often wielded by those a leader surrounds themselves with because some have only gravitated to their position for the station itself. Having a subtle delivery and control over 'tipping your hand' will often plant your idea in a person's head, letting them come to your conclusion.

Be careful employing such tactics in a manipulative or heavy-handed way. It should be a matter of laying out facts and how those interconnect, not you leading someone around by the nose. Real leaders talk about Forming Consensus and Building Bridges; when wielding power by personal whim rather than mutual accord, the leader becomes the dictator. But we will talk about the power of compromise in-depth further on. Suffice to say, know yourself and the person you are talking to, and asserting yourself becomes a matter of finding a path together rather than wrestling someone into submission.

Focus

Keeping your eyes on the prize can be challenging, and we usually cannot maintain intense concentration for long. Getting distracted is easy, and sometimes it even helps to walk away from something we are looking closely at to gain perspective. However, in a persuasive conversation, this equates to "circling back" to a topic, having allowed it to stray. Practice and a little forethought will enable you to guide the aside or tangent toward matters that relate to your goal, tying it together to emphasize the point. Someone truly skilled at assertiveness will even be able to turn a rebuttal around and spin a No into a Maybe.

To learn this, practice rejoinder statements, retorts, and comebacks, which are positive but turn around a denial. "Great!" and "I agree" are wonderful turnabout words; follow them up with a reasonable alternative. For instance, you are trying to sell someone on something. It could be a literal sale or just going to the restaurant of your choice, but the person is balking.

"I just don't have the money for eating at X right now."

"I agree. That's why we go during happy hour and share an entree."

or

"I can't make that decision without talking to my partner."

"Great! We'll get them on the phone!"

It sounds weird at first and feels so forced the first time you do it, but after you try it a few times, you will find it is an effective gambit and works because people generally want to be liked and get along with others. As I mentioned earlier on, if you can form a strong enough retort, you can make the other person feel they came to a conclusion themselves. The movie Inception played with this idea:

some people will automatically reject an idea they didn't come up with themselves. You just cannot tell some people anything, so laying a trail of breadcrumbs becomes your only resource. Mastering the "soft-sell" in sales or being a persuasive friend in life, sticking to logic and reason as much as possible will pay off. As long as like-minded people surround you, you can even layout a bunch of facts and sit back, letting everyone else put it together themselves.

We have talked a good deal now about how to remain above your emotions while still heeding them. I mentioned how important it is to key into the emotional state of the people you are with, so you are not rubbing them the wrong way and can more easily appeal to their sensibilities. Empathy and sympathy are no small tasks, and in the next chapter, I will go over exactly how you convey an open mind and receptive ear while not losing yourself. In the meantime, though, make sure and take a look at your interpersonal dealings and decide if you need to change how you redirect and control situations.

Do you assert your will at all? At work or school, are you a cork on the surface of a river? Being tossed this way and that, no direction and at the whim of the forces surrounding you? Granted, as a pupil or employee, it can be challenging, if not simply a bad idea, to try asserting yourself too much. How about socially? Do you supply input in group decisions or just do what everyone else does? Humans have a reasonably inherent need to express themselves: do you give yourself that opportunity? Do you give your friends and loved ones a chance to call the shots?

Knowing your place and knowing where you stand will aid you immeasurably, and even champions of industry and world leaders know when to give a little.

Chapter 5: Step 5 - Active Listening

Body language, eye contact, repeating what another said in your own words, and tone all play a *massive* part in how effective your communication will be. How to assert yourself more effectively. That shifts the focus. While we still have to make sure our body is telling the speaker we are actively listening, now we are looking at how we can be more intentional in what those cues are broadcasting.

Because if we can show the person we hear them, that we're not just waiting for our turn to talk but have taken their words into account, they will be more inclined to consider it. Mostly, people just want to be heard. When pushing your agenda and someone objects, frequently, that objection is based on nothing more than the person being objectionable. Meet their gaze, nod your head, agree they have a point, or at the very least tell them you understand why they feel the way they do before launching into your counterpoint.

Me, Myself, and Eye

Eye Contact, in the context of active listening, is more important than your body language. "Eyes up front!" gets shouted from the fronts of classrooms, and putting your finger on your nose while searching for eye contact is a popular way to regain focus when among friends. Even if you are seated side by side, looking over at the person talking, at least in glances, makes sure they know your investment in what they are saying. People know you won't back down when you keep eye contact. You will notice that when a person is ready to give in, they avert their eyes and sometimes often quite literally throw their hands up in defeat!

Eye contact is so important because it's hardwired right into our brains. Hold someone's eyes too long, and you go from 'visibly passionate' to 'intimidating.' Wide eyes denote excitement, interest in the speaker's words, but if they are too wide for too long, you look like a maniac. We are so inclined to track where a person is looking because we have a dedicated center of the visual part of our brain just for eyes. You can make great apes in a zoo attack the glass between you by baring your teeth and locking eyes with them; that instinct remains, so be extra careful when you start experimenting with keeping a gaze.

One word of reassurance: no one is looking at you the way you look at yourself. Even your mom or partner isn't scrutinizing your every utterance and gesture. I don't know who out there needed to hear that, but there you are. Go ahead and "dance like no one is watching" because usually, they aren't!

Practice a bit of ocular awareness: where are you looking when someone is talking? Where are you looking when you are talking?

Body Language

How we say something is more important than the words themselves, as long as you include facial expressions in that definition. Convey you are listening, demonstrate understanding, and otherwise let the person or people know you have not only heard but listened to them. You will have done more towards your assertiveness in the situation than if you had delivered a passionate speech. Humans were social animals first, and that drive to feel included is strong. Include people with your actions and tone, if not direct words; many introverts and shy people need a little coaxing.

When delivering questions to a group, eyeball the person who never speaks up. If you continuously offer suggestions or examples when the group discusses, why not try remaining silent? Please don't pull a turtle out of its shell, but you can certainly entice a reticent person to engage with engagement and open-ended questions. Nothing is more flattering than questions about yourself because even the self-effacing or humble want to share a little. We go into exactly how we use words further on. For now, think about your stance. Good posture is not only good for the back and body but social bearing, too.

Your face tells a lot about your emotional state, and so much humor is based on irony and inverting the truth that "your kidding!" has become a way of saying "no way!" Make sure your face is on the same page as your mouth. Lies reveal themselves through our "tells," little unconscious pieces of behavior that everyone has and is picked up on, even unconsciously, by those around us. People who spend enough time around us learn these ticks and habits and consciously or intuitively will come to know you as an honest person or a two-faced one.

Restate

Repeating what the other person said verbatim isn't good enough, usually. When you take the content of what someone has said and say it back to them in your own words, you leave no room for doubt that you understood them. This confirmation is validating and makes sure that when you disagree with them, they know it is not because you do not understand their point. Asserting yourself is more manageable when everyone affected feels heard; as long as you have demonstrated understanding and compassion in the past, they will feel that you at least took their position into account. It would be best if you were doing this anyway.

If you are guilty of not listening and just waiting for the other person to shut up so you can talk again, then it is homework time. Do not take all the air out of a conversation, and even if you are "the smartest person in the room," I guarantee other people have valuable points of view.

The surer you are that you are always right, the more on guard you should now be that you are, in fact, sometimes wrong.

Have I mentioned already that nobody is right all the time? Fear not, I address this in detail further on, but for the sake of active listening skills, I invite you to take in what people are saying to you, really let divergent ideas roll around in your head. Walking in another's shoes gives you insights and understanding that nothing else can, but you have to look at their experience without bias or judgment.

Again, though, we are sometimes stuck with needing to understand another's opinion if only so we might change it or at least learn to stand opposed to it. Because at the end of the day, if you can't assert your will enough to sway someone's feelings, you should at least remain faithful to yours. All of this deep understanding comes with a responsibility, though. Once we see a different option and it is better than the one we have, we owe ourselves the opportunity for positive change. The other side of the No One Is Right All The Time formula is We Have To Change Our Minds Sometimes.

Assuming you are the one who wants to do the convincing, it is time we looked at the power of "I." The quote made famous in Spiderman, "With great power comes great responsibility," predates Stan Lee by a few centuries, but it is as accurate now as it was in the bronze age. Learning how to assert yourself can be even more influential than persuasion. The strength of assertiveness over persuasiveness is because the former is mainly passive. "Assert" is something you do to yourself, while "Persuade" is active, something you are doing to someone else. You can "fly in under the radar" of many people's defenses. If you've come this far, you owe it to yourself to master the follow-through.

Empathy

Active listening is processing the things people are saying as they say them. That includes attempting to Feel the other person, too. "I feel you" is a wonderful little modern shorthand, an acknowledgment that you share the other person's emotional state.

Be sure you observe the difference between Sympathy and Empathy. Sympathy is when you begin crying when other people are crying, laugh when they laugh and feel angry when they are; empathy knows *why* they are feeling those things, understanding what elicited these feelings but not giving in to them yourself. Tied up as it is in mirror neurons and the endocrine system, psychology, and upbringing, every one of us have differing levels. Getting swept away by other people's emotional state makes it harder to help, to say nothing of more difficult to regulate ourselves.

Practice empathy; if you are somewhat remote, have a hard time "keying in" to the inner life of others, or otherwise possess a great deal of apathy, your project is to start trying to. Usually, with a family member or loved one, you can start by saying, "how was your day?" or "how are you feeling?" with direct eye contact and leaning your upper body slightly toward the person and *really* listening to them. All too often, we use those kinds of statements as a substitute for "hello" or "good day!"; that's why you have to add body language to indicate you are actually interested.

On the other hand, if you suffer from a surfeit of empathy, if you are one of those individuals for whom the emotional state of others rings like a bell in your ear, I invite you to practice taking the emotions of others as passively as you can. Water off a duck's back- to observe but not participate. Again, it can feel like these reactions are so instinctual as to be out of your control. But you can recondition yourself in lots of ways, your sensitivity and emotional responses included.

When it comes to listening instead of hearing, understanding rather of learning, and replying with consideration instead of rote reactions, we enable more robust, profound levels of communication but also risk taking on too much. A little piece of Eastern-inspired poetry gives me an image full of symbolic meaning I like to hold in my mind's eye when the going gets tough.

"I am the stone in the river. I move the river; the river does not move me. White water takes away my sharp edges; makes me smooth. Yet I remain whole." Maybe it only works because it forces me to imagine a river, and nature is scientifically proven to lower stress hormones in the body.

We acknowledge the feelings of others, their validity, and the right of the other person to feel them (within reason), but we do not let them into ourselves unless we want to. Boundaries, remember?

Chapter 6: Step 6 - Validate Others' Feelings

"Validating people" has been a buzzword in recent decades, so much so that there is now an undercurrent of not validating everyone. Do you give participation trophies or only reward the high-achievers? On a smaller scale, do you praise, compliment, and welcome everyone regardless, or withhold accolades and respect until something special is accomplished or a bond is formed? Why reward average behavior? Why wait until a triumph to give a reward?

Sound biology and experiential data support positive reinforcement, that's why.

Validating People

When it comes time to go on the offensive, you lob "attacks" as softly as you can. Because all stick and no carrot quite simply will not be tolerated in this age. The human-animal is more susceptible to lasting change when its pleasure centers are engaged rather than our fight/flight responses. Our synapses even track shouts of delight and laughter ever so slightly faster than pain and fear; he has evolved to seek joy.

So many people still labor under the delusion that you can whip people into shape. Whether you are talking about actual corporal punishment or just yelling and threatening people, the result is the same. A beat dog might not attack you, but it will not do much else for you, either. Again and again, I see people defend hitting their kids because that is how their parents raised them, and it made them reliable, disciplined, tough, or any number of supposed benefits. My response is always the same.

Did you turn out OK, though? Are you balanced and happy, really? How much better would you have been without pain and intimidation from a loved one used as a discipline? As we come to understand just how little it takes for the human brain to go through Post Traumatic Stress Disorder, the less reason we have ever to strike anyone, who is not actively trying to attack us, I suppose!

Reward the desired behavior and (within reason) ignore the bad. Redirect, distract or otherwise get past unwanted behavior. Be careful, of course, in exerting too much. In children, it's easy to change the subject quickly, but adults are likely to take offense. Again, unless you have established a baseline of trust and kindness from someone we know takes our feelings into account and confidence to honor our sensibilities, we receive even pointed objections with an open mind.

Own your words, don't put them into other people's heads.

"No, you're wrong" is a slap in the face. "I feel you're wrong" is at least a little better. It is tempting to say "have you ever considered..."

as a rebuttal, but even that has the triggering word You in it. "What I have learned…" or something that retains ownership of the idea will be a less threatening way of communicating. Remember, we are not giving in, we are still pushing, but we will not make the listener feel attacked, defensive, or even directly challenged.

Passive Aggressive is this style of soft-sell taken too far. We are learning how to assert ourselves, not sitting back and sniping at people.

I used the metaphor of a turtle in its shell earlier, and the biases and reactionary responses humans employ to deal with day-to-day life are just as reflexive. When people feel poked, prodded, or manipulated, they shut down, pulling into their shell. You could be on fire, and if the person with a bucket of water said, "Are you stupid, who lights themselves on fire?" it might take a second to accept their help! Extreme? Maybe. But in the primitive, evolutionary action/reaction of the unconscious mind, your feelings don't have to make sense. But you do have to live with them.

Are you angry all the time? Anger releases the same hormones as fear, which is why it is so easy to flip from afraid to angry. Nobody likes to feel scared, so that pushes even more anger. Anger also gives you a little dopamine, and anything which triggers dopamine has a greater than average chance of becoming addicting. I know some people hate the idea that addiction is more a disease than a behavior, or even that it is possible to become addicted to behavior at all. Decades of study have born that out, however. There is a genetic piece of the compulsion puzzle, and some people are more susceptible to becoming hooked on certain substances than others. Addiction itself can be a problem for an unlucky percentage of the population, the so-called "addictive personality" a matter of heredity as much as temperament. You lose the ability to assert yourself when addiction is asserting itself for you.

If you find yourself seeking out things that make you angry, looking for the next hit of rage, I offer an alternative. You can still get what you need without getting it from sources that play on your emotions. The Information Age has muddied the waters too thoroughly. Someone with a love of emotional arousal needs to look no further than the 24-hour news cycle. Old school journalism answers "The Five Ws" and little else: who, what, where, when, and why. Modern profit-hungry news outlets follow drama and pain. If it bleeds, it leads, and if there's no one bleeding, you run around looking for blood.

Because simply 'not watching (or reading, or listening to) the news is a terrible solution. We learn, and we grow, or we stagnate and wither. If you realize you are on the wrong side of something in the course of preparing to debate someone, you are in great company. On the other hand, to be wishy-washy is to surrender all opinions to those around you or change your mind every time you get new information.

Do Not Be Manipulated

Put simply: if the source of information is telling you how to feel, it is manipulative.

Asserting yourself begins and ends with being responsive. In ages past, it was enough that an authority figure was, well, an authority figure: people respected the office, obeyed rules and norms simply by virtue of the person having a position of power. You can't expect to lead people simply because it is in your job description in the modern age. Seniority means nothing if you do not have their respect. Even if you worked your way up in an organization and gained leadership through achievement, you cannot rely on your reputation to precede you. Though everyone knows you and your ability, if you start barking orders and forget to listen, it will be as if you are a different person.

Balancing a tough-as-nails attitude *and* flexible, even changeable of mind, is a lifelong process. Traditionally, the older we get, the more set rigid we become. Change is the only fundamental constant in the universe. Innovation can be troubling unless you have learned how to bend or at least when to ignore it. But if the modern age of social division and personal isolation has demonstrated anything, it is that we are stronger together. Even if you dislike the group, in some cases, divide and conquer is far too effective to separate yourself from the whole.

Appeal to People's Better Halves

Master the 'compliment sandwich,' couching any negative statements or feedback in more positive comments. Stating the bad with the good in a way that doesn't upset the person only works if you have established a baseline of kindness or neutrality. If you are constantly issuing commands and offering critical advice, then suddenly, come in with complement-critique-complement, it will sound phony and rehearsed. Even so! If it comes across as stagy, it will be better than if you had made no effort at all.

Because, again, it comes down to people wanting to see that effort. Make a person feel that you actively consider their opinion, and you will be more successful in acting against it.

Being supple of mind, allowing ourselves the opportunity to mature, adapt, and change requires the ability to receive those kinds of critiques, too. I am using polite language, but critical statements, more often than not, don't feel like a critique: a carefully worded deconstruction of your work by a mentor. No, many are delivered in anger, using harsh words thrown without thought. Most comments we receive as a judgment were never intended to slight or hurt but resulted from an off-hand or inconsiderate remark. Learning how to look at negative language and decide if we will let it affect us is key to personal growth.

After all, that blowhard jerk who bawled you out and made a rude gesture while honking this morning might be harsh, but *were* you in error? Sometimes someone's poor delivery of information can be so antagonistic we simply shrug and say, "what an ass!" without considering if they might have a point. Cognitive bias and the human reactionary response being what it is, we tend to defend ANY behavior we have held long enough, even if we know it is negative.

Do They Have a Point?

Just as I say, "you should be analyzing even negative input for value," I know there's so much misinformation, opinion presented as fact, and plain old mean people there are out there you really should not. You *have* to keep those defenses up, but you cannot lock yourself behind stone, either. Develop those defenses, too, if you lack them.

In our efforts to validate someone's feelings, we have to make sure we don't lose our own. But sometimes, our feelings are dumb. As much as we'd love to believe our every intuitive urge is coming from our higher mind, just as often as not, it is primitive, base instincts or emotional reactions we developed when we were babies. Remember, we have to be capable of reflecting on the integrity of our ideas if we hope to lead with them or stick to them. If based on feelings alone, it may be fear, hate, or envy.

With a handle on our motivations, we have to ask ourselves IF asserting ourselves in a situation is even a good idea. Leading, even just supplying good ideas, can be just as addicting as any strong feeling, and being on guard against such self-serving agendas will make sure those you serve feel they are in good hands. I say Serve because leaders must acknowledge their responsibility for everyone under them, not only the direction everyone is going. In the next chapter, we focus on the power of compromise, the result of all we have learned in this one.

To wrap up this section, we remember to not only observe others' feelings but to be mindful of our own. I liken our emotions to a river we need to cross; mind it, tend to it, or it will sweep you away.

Chapter 7: Step 7 - Compromise

Sometimes giving ground is the stronger choice. Winning doesn't always look like taking 1st Place, especially when looking at the big picture. We hear the metaphor "sometimes you have to sacrifice a pawn," but I prefer "two steps forward, one step back." I'm not particularly eager to sacrifice anything if I can help it, but I'll happily let someone take the larger share if there's a long-term goal involved. Many of us are so competitive that we lose for winning. That means we get so caught up in coming out on top we step on toes, make bitter enemies out of innocent rivals, and otherwise let our obsession with always being the victor blind us to over-arching objectives.

Take all parties' needs into account and nobody feels ignored or used. There is no greater skill a leader can have than balancing the needs of the whole with the needs of the individuals. Many people in a leadership position take the My Way or the Highway approach, believe they know best no matter what, and direct the group with no input from anyone. While this may work, you'll never land as close to the mark if you don't consult, throw ideas back and forth, or at least ask for input. Even if everyone's thoughts fall short of what's needed and you have to ignore them, if challenged, as long as you considered it, you'll have a clear response as to why you did something else.

In an interpersonal decision, compromise becomes even more critical. Groups are easier to disappear in, though leading one varies from "herding cats" to "impossible." The smaller the group, the more individuals in it are going to want agency over decisions made. Reflection on your boundaries and talking about them often will help: compromise need not always give something if the other party is interested in something else. Be honest, forthright (speaking your intention without beating around the bush), and fair, and I think you'll find most people are willing to flex as long as you treat them fairly.

Choice, Options and Feedback

Often, you'll not even need to compromise as long as you offer people some customization. People want to feel heard. They want to feel appreciated and recognized. Most people do not want to make the shots; they want a say in what you shoot. Usually, there is more than one path to victory, so letting those with you help decide the way forward is a good idea. Be sure you research and truly understand the forces surrounding a situation first. Many facilitators have lost the group's focus because the discussion was open, and a new idea got everyone carried away.

If you *know* a specific course of action is the only way to go, offer those affected a way to add their personal touch. This isn't the same as Illusion of Choice but an honest attempt to make people feel comfortable with a choice that was out of their hands. Personalizing an impersonal request can be practically anything, but it should be tangible, something the person can see or touch, if not intangible, like a public thanks.

As long as you gather feedback, act on it as much as possible, and be respectful, everyone should be OK. Adults have to learn at some point that life is a long series of compromises, and things seldom work out exactly as we'd like. Sometimes the Suggestion Box is a valuable insight into the group's needs; sometimes, everything has already been decided, and the suggestions go right in the trash. Even if things are locked in, taking the time to read those suggestions or talk to your group with sincerity and honesty will give you insight into what people are thinking.

Because frequently, Mamma DOES Know Best. Compromise is not always possible, the die is set, and there is nothing to be done even if you wanted to. Whether you're socializing or holding a summit meeting, allowing people to make a decision, even when the result is a foregone conclusion, will ensure everyone is happy with the result.

Illusion of Choice

This is a trick employed by parents all the time, and it can be terribly transparent if used clumsily, but its ability to get a job done is legendary. You present multiple options in its most straightforward setup, but all of them lead back to a single result. Imagine a flowchart or mind-map: you have a single destination you are trying to get to but multiple paths there. Set up this kind of converging network of selections imaginatively, and you will know success. Asserting yourself in this way should be exercised with caution, however, as it is in no uncertain terms, a trick.

Do you want to pay taxes at the end of the year or a little bit at a time? It is a choice, but in either case, you still pay. Would you like carrots, broccoli, or corn? In all cases, you've eaten a vegetable.

State the choices as stand-alone decisions as much as you can, don't be arbitrary but let people pick things about which they care. Some people are picky about food, while others simply could not care less. Make sure you poll before you begin getting people to decide because you may come to find you are the only person with a strong opinion, and you are dithering yourself out of something that never needed a vote in the first place.

Stronger Together

Ultimately, the point of compromise isn't to get your way. It is to get everyone's way. If everyone affected by a conclusion can supply input during the decision-making phase, the result will be far more palatable than if the call was made from a so-called ivory tower. Since no one is always right, the effect will be more substantial, too. You have to make sure the opinions weighed are well-informed ones, of course. Feedback from someone who knows nothing of the subject or demonstrated poor judgment in the past doesn't do anyone any favors. It is appeasing those who shouldn't be listened to at all that makes Illusion of Choice a viable option. In groups of children, the naive or ignorant, it does not pay to equally take all points of view. If you sensed a "but" coming up, your intuition was sharp.

Don't Take Advice From Fools is a classic adage; however, this cliche is troubled by the fact that one so seldom realizes one's own short-comings (it is hard to know what you don't know!), we can never really say for sure who's words should have more weight than any other. Since everyone has a unique point-of-view and true wisdom comes from appreciating the perspective of everyone, it is never in your best interests to ignore someone entirely.

The plurality of voice is the essence of democracy in a nation and love in a friendship. When everyone's needs are as important as the needs of the self, when we decide to assert ourselves, we choose to lead. Leading ourselves or leading our nation, it doesn't matter what scale you are looking at: asserting yourself is a powerful tool. Standing for what we believe in, knowing when to update our beliefs, and staying true or inspiring others is all we have to gain.

Conclusion

Making some of these inner changes can be the most arduous undertaking we have ever undertaken. Changing how you interact with the world and how you interact with yourself is some serious homework. Sometimes it will seem daunting. Other times we will backslide or relapse into old patterns. We strive forward as hard and as far as we can for precisely this reason: if you lose ground, it will hopefully not set you back to square one. Two steps forward, one back; being aggressive in your personal changes if nothing else will take you far.

Aggression has no place in interpersonal communication. Anger and hostility are counter-productive at best and only aid in undermining a leader's actual authority. If you begin to fight, you have already lost. There is quite simply no room for aggressive confrontation in the modern world. Thwarting active violence against your person notwithstanding, of course, your fiery emotionalism and two-fisted passion will only work for you if you can channel that heat into something constructive.

Let your feelings be a forge, not a conflagration.

Make sure what you believe serves you and doesn't hold you back. We live our lives striving and growing or begin to wither and die. We spend our childhood learning with such wide-eyed enthusiasm it can be overwhelming to the adults around us. As we mature, we choose a focus or two. By the time we retire, many of us seem to have stopped learning altogether. The death of imagination and curiosity is often the death of our ability to lead effectively. Once we cut ourselves off from the input of the people around us, we lose the ability to make informed decisions.

If this guide has taught you anything, I hope that is the reflection and change part. So many of us labor under this delusion that a strong leader just LEADS and we should just follow. But history and experience demonstrate the most influential leaders are the ones who are talking to not only their peers but listening to those they command, as well. No Man Is An Island should be evident to anyone: we don't stand alone. We can't stand alone. After all, humanity is a social creature, but we are a tribe of equals, not a hive under a queen.

So go forth with a firmer understanding of how to assert yourself in any situation. With a smile and a well-informed opinion. Know when to change and when to be the force of change. Know when to remain as you are. More and more, the Information Age has proven to be as much about folklore, what you *want* to be true and passionately brandished opinions as it has been about facts and data.

In the still calm center of your heart or the swirling mass of a crowd, a hard, almost unmovable center and malleable, ductile facade will give you the agility and flexibility to meet any challenge head-on.

Book 2: Social Skills

7 Easy Steps to Master Emotional Intelligence, Making Friends, Relationship Building & Interpersonal Skills

Lawrence Finnegan

Introduction

Welcome to "Social Skills". In this guide, we'll teach you how to put some of the final pieces of a happy, healthy life in place. Humans are social creatures, and ignoring the "sense of belonging" is like ignoring your sense of smell.

Modern life is pretty splintered in the 2020s. More so than any other point in my life, people are holed up in their homes, factionalized and isolated. Since the modern age, the industrialized world has always had a lush, thriving collection of subcultures. The term "subculture" itself is a misnomer, as any group identified as "sub-" most likely doesn't think of itself as beneath. Indeed, due to the before mentioned splitting, even the middle seems strangely at odds with itself.

The time has never been better to look at what binds humanity together and how we can apply that to our lives. When people concern themselves with better social skills, society benefits as much as the individual; take these lessons to heart, think of socializing as a skill you work out like a muscle group, and let's get physical.

Let's get started!

Chapter 1: Step 1 - Work on You

Beyond the basics, grooming, posture, and body language, you have to ask yourself what *exactly* you want from society at large. What do you hope to achieve by sharpening your interpersonal communication skills? Of course, we will be going over a few specific goals, namely casual, intimate, and business, but you might have something in particular in mind. Wherever possible, I have attempted to be as conceptual as possible, deconstructing the lessons to make sure you can use parts, if not the whole. Social skills are the most far-reaching and foundational of all the life skills you can learn. Humans have demonstrated again and again that we are stronger together.

Balance and Reciprocity

You don't have to be beautiful to be attractive; it helps, of course, but if you can't captivate or at least engage, no amount of grooming and good genes will create lasting bonds. I have heard it said, "you have to love yourself before anyone else can love you," and that's garbage. It is perfectly possible to love someone who doesn't love themselves, but the danger there is an asymmetric love, a lopsided relationship of "all take, no give" or "all push no pull." Balance and reciprocity are the rules of a solid social bond, fleeting or lasting.

Inspire people to assume the best when meeting you by always having your best foot forward. Let's make sure you are someone people *want* to approach or be approached by!

Basic Self Care

It may be through no fault of your own that these lessons got skipped. Maybe you were like me and raised by a wolf, er, hard-working single father, who loved us and supported us but *may* have missed a few finishing touches. Maybe your hard work has pushed some of these simple steps aside. Whatever the case, take a moment to consider your daily routine and how it leaves you in the world.

No vanity, egotism, or any kind of mirror gazing is required. Get enough sleep, wash, eat and clothe yourself reasonably and call it good. If make-up and fashion are essential to you, you might dedicate as much energy to it as you like, but any more than an hour *tops* is pushing what is expected of a mere mortal. If you do indulge, either for professional or personal style, just be aware of how the time required affects your relationships: people will only accuse you of being "high-maintenance" or a "diva" if *they* are inconvenienced by it.

Sleep

Sleep is so darn important that I have to assume you know if it's a problem for you. If you are not getting at least seven to eight hours of sleep a night, erring on the side of eight, you are selling yourself short.

Re-form a nighttime routine to get that needed rest. Not only do you get energy for the next day, but long-term memory and learning are improved, too; remembering names and details from the past are all keys to lasting social connections.

Sleeping together undoubtedly makes people closer, though how the rest of the relationship progresses will depend on how you deal with intimacy.

Eating Well

Eating good leaves you with enough energy and focus to last an entire conversation. Again, this is a simple thing, but adults just *love* to think the time saved by not eating will be well spent. Some hunger symptoms are tight-lipped tension ("hangry") or being overly chatty and friendly. Unfortunately for the "overly chatty and friendly" one, your social filter is usually dropped as well, and you have to consciously remind yourself not just to say whatever comes to mind; I know that one all too well.

Of course, eating together is as famous a friend-maker as drinking together, so don't be afraid to make lunch groups if asking a single person feels weird.

Grooming

Grooming is about how it makes you feel as much as it makes sure you're not stinky or messy. Standards have shifted toward low upkeep, so observe the basics and consider the rest optional. Same with

68

clothes; you have to be part of the in-group before telling the difference between punks and artists versus the homeless or transient. Most folks get by with one shower or bath a day, and as long as you're not working up a sweat, that's fine. Deodorant or antiperspirant will make sure the effects last as long as possible. If your clothes are old or don't reflect you as a person, ditch them.

Shopping together, beauty appointments, and trading hygiene secrets are great bonding experiences. Hair maintenance, especially, seems to engender a willingness to chat and socialize.

Look Good, Feel Good I have said it a few times now, but let me articulate it in no uncertain terms: we groom for *them* second after doing it for ourselves. While we feel about how we look is based mainly on cultural symbols and trends, it must also be about how we think and what we want. A tidy room makes you feel calm and allows you to think, just like fresh clothes after getting clean, you feel renewed and capable. We signal the type of people we want to attract, and just as much as any peacock, bower bird, or penguin, our displays and nests demonstrate our capability and willingness to work for kinship.

A few interpersonal basics which I see lacking in adults again and again:

- Take "no" for an answer
- Let others talk
- Actively listen
- Respect boundaries

Drives and Motivations

Why do you want to form or expand your social network? Yes, I realize we all have an instinctual urge to band up and enjoy the company of our fellow humans, but what, specifically, do you get from it?

Look at how you interact with the people you know; consider your contributions as well as anything they may do for you. "Give and take" can be as trivial as listening to you complain about work or as significant as helping you move; appreciate that everyone is the star in their own movie. Do you seek friends? A lover? Lovers?

Acquaintance, Friend or Lover

A large pool of casual acquaintances is a good starting point, but with no depth to any of your relationships, it can begin to feel almost as lonely as none at all. School, work, and any regular gathering of strangers create instant *familiarity*, which the word "family" roots with good reason. Besides our parents, we all begin as strangers to each other, and it is only through a long process of opening up that we

70

allow those random faces to become beloved friends or our favorite family.

The growth of a friend into a best friend is organic and should not be rushed. You can do a few things to hurry the process, but there are no shortcuts to human socialization.

Because family isn't just about blood but bonds, and while we have a biological family, we also have a logical one. So, having made sure we know what we want and have put our best foot forward, let's look at where we're walking.

It's essential to feel at ease wherever you go, which can also be developed.

Date Yourself

If you feel weird eating out alone, then you have to. Same going to a movie, or anything solo. You have a right to feel comfortable in your skin. Own the space you're in. When we are young, it is crucial to surround ourselves with friends. Friendships are an important part of how we form identities. Many of us never grow out of needing constant contact, and others let everyone drift away. College and then career come and go, with days busy and nights full. We hit post-college or mid-life, and suddenly, everyone is focused on their families or just drifted into their own life. Unless we have developed a strong sense of self, we find ourselves isolated and depressed. Of course, picking up a book on developing social skills can help get you back out there, but relying on other people to fulfill you All the Time is not healthy, either.

You want a strong friendship with yourself first, so foster positive self-talk as well as good hygiene.

Balance, in all things, is key to long-term happiness. The focus here *is* on making connections so let's stop navel-gazing, turn without, and cast our gaze instead upon the world.

Chapter 2: Step 2 - Understand Them

You're looking good and feeling good: your clothes reflect how you want to be seen as well as your personal style; you do not smell or appear upset. The time has come to decide who to approach and who to let approach you. While we always honor the individualism of people, we recognize that much of our identities come from outside stimuli. Even the most eccentric boundary pusher is reacting against society, which is to say even anarchists care enough to want change. Once we identify what forces have gathered a group together, it becomes easier to join that group.

Stick to what you love. Interest groups cover anything you can imagine and more: once you begin to explore and dig deep, you'll discover cliques within subgroups you never even imagined. Don't be afraid of getting into something new just because the people look interesting. Chances are, if you think people look intriguing or exciting, you'll find a common thread if not shared interest. Like attracts like, and no matter one's surface, if you share a favored trait, that will be enough to foster a bond. Even exclusive organizations recruit, and social groups are social for a reason.

There Is No THEM

Take a note from transcendental philosophies and acknowledge that we are all one: there is *far* more in common between one another than not. A big part of getting over your fear of making new contacts is knowing most folks want a relationship, too. A creeping feeling of isolation has crept into many of our lives, and it is past time we got out and made some moves. We are wolves in the night, howling, hoping we are not alone.

Many times we talk ourselves out of walking over and saying "hi" because we've watched too much media or were raised by toxic parents- mean people are rare; most of us will at least be kind, if not open to friendly overtures. Maybe the negative self-talk began with toxic loved ones or is simply chemical. Whatever the reason you have been holding yourself back, we now must ask ourselves what kinds of people we want in our lives. When we look at ourselves honestly, it becomes readily apparent what types of people we want to surround ourselves with.

What Do You Stand For?

Philosophically, it is dangerous to define yourself by what you are against. Look at what you like, what drives you. It may not be even so profound as religion or spirituality; many creative personalities group up around their favored pursuit, and the internet has made it even easier to find like-minded folks. Pro sports have sponsors, which means a built-in social scene. Most cities of any size have an Art Walk where galleries and studios are open to the public. Conventions, the Meet-Ups website, and others like it all focus individuals into a single location.

Of course, religion has served this role for millennia, and we have a plurality of them here- if one disappointed you, maybe try finding another?

Remember that going to a large public gathering for the first time alone gives you the freedom to check things out at your own speed and leave if you want to without pressure.

Demographics Vs. Individuals

We can't pigeonhole people, which is to say label folks, and then limit our expectations to that bias. Neither do we usually have the mental bandwidth to take everyone as individuals all the time. Prejudice is, at the root of it all, the brain's way of saving energy, a cognitive shorthand our pattern obsessed brain uses to make sense of the world.

On the one hand, it is OK because humans tend to group, form cliques and subgroups all by ourselves. On the other, if you let yourself mistake the group label for an identity, then you've just sold everyone short, including yourself.

Simply knowing that not everyone in the demographic identifies with it is enough. There are some anti-feminist women, senior citizens who do everything possible to turn from Golden Years culture, and you had better *not* identify a teen as a kid; or an adult- you know what, don't label teens anything at all (they have it covered). Kidding aside, even in the demographics one has a choice in, the reason for being there can differ significantly.

Why Are They Here?

Consider a sci-fi convention as a lurid example. Yes, you have the core group there for the media in question. But you have people who like cosplay, unpaid custom making, science enthusiasts interested in the ideas brought up, gawkers and hawkers, and artists of all kinds.

Knitting circles used to be the exclusive domain of old ladies, but lately, younger people and men have been getting into crochet and other related hobbies. Again, the interest varies from wanting to make stuff out of yarn to the process of tying knots into shapes to the perceived irony of young people and/or males doing something outside the norm itself. Even "guerrilla crochet groups" make random, usually anonymous public installations in funny or provocative places overnight. You can bet the motivation of those groups is not what motivated your grandma Phyllis to make mom's quilt.

Follow Your Bliss

We don't always get a chance to do what we love for a living. Even those of us working in fields we enjoy have work to do. Lack of freedom over your day is why it is so important to pursue our ends in your personal life. Don't let expectations or societal pressures force you into relationships you hate. Not casual and certainly not intimate. Ideally, you shouldn't hate your job anyway and if fate and fortune have conspired to place you in a situation you hate, having a solid social life is all the more critical.

Find the people who stimulate you and keep their company. A good conversation should charge you up, give you ideas and draw out the best in you. Identify the people who are constantly cutting you down, taking but never giving, and otherwise drain you and get them out of your life. Again, if fate and circumstance force someone into your life who takes too much, ration them or cut them off entirely. Being a good friend maintains **healthy boundaries**, so never be afraid to put your foot down when you notice an imbalance.

Scenes, Haunts & Social Locale

Music: You can enjoy music, play music, or write music. Making and writing music have the built-in social element of collaboration, though you can still do it solo- get out and share! Jam and collaborate; mix and fusion. Those of us on the outside can just stand back and enjoy. Dancing or otherwise watching music is a great focus to meet around, but it is often too loud and dark to meet people. Still, a lot of life before, after-parties, the edge of the crowd, and the performers' social media are all excellent places to meet like minds, to say nothing of seeing someone with a T-shirt or patch and calling it out.

The smaller a performer's following, the more excited we tend to be when meeting another fan "in the wild," half the point of band merch as cultural identity signaling. This carries over to practically every interest, hobby, and thought-group you can imagine: the more particular, niche, or small the interest group is, the more welcoming they tend to be of curious outsiders. With a few notable exceptions, groups want new members and will happily accommodate if not recruit fresh faces.

Beyond the Bar

Booze is the "easy button" of socializing; its ability to become a problem, getting too loose, and annual expense are all reasons one might want to forgo the club, bar or other liquor fueled pursuits.

Coffee, tea, and quick snack stops of all kinds abound, though you might want to be a familiar face before you make casual approaches. Frequent the venue, "haunt" it as they say. We tend to have our guard up when just darting in and out, so if you're going to socialize at a coffee place or restaurant, make sure it is in the seating area or someone similarly at leisure. You can charm your way past that initial ice on most of us, though always be mindful of non-verbal cues: some people are passive and have difficulty expressing negative feelings.

I mentioned hobbies and interest groups, but you can think broader than that. The information age has ushered in an era where practically ANY idea has a group focused around it. This is why it is important to define what you stand for instead of what you are against. At worst, this is literally a hate group; at best, you will pass the stress and agitation around in a bleak circle jerk. If you are upset enough to stand against something, find a way to work toward its solution. In other words, find constructive, positive ways to thwart what vexes you.

Express Yourself

Why would I place this section at the end of Understand Them, well after Work on You? Because the self-expression I am talking about is the type that broadcasts something of our personality. It need not be any "thing" at all but could be your style itself. Some people will not need this lesson and might even want to rein it in. If *every* article of clothing you wear is a statement piece, you might be a teenager. That is not even humor, as the years between the onset of puberty and our prefrontal cortex firming up are generally times of trying new things and personal exploration.

If you *never* gave yourself the chance to try different dress styles, modes, and even demeanors, it is never too late to reinvent yourself. Call it on a mid-life crisis or golden age renaissance because nobody will care if you change up how you dress and talk until your early thirties.

Nobody thinks about you the way you think about yourself. Beyond the occasional saint or devoted loved one, you can just relax and do what you like because the heavy scrutiny many of us labor under does not exist. We are all the main characters in our own stories. A trick of perception makes the world literally revolve around each and every one of us. The best of us observe the illusion and try not to dominate and influence every encounter we possibly can.

Chapter 3: Step 3 - Make Small Talk Big

So much is made of inclusion and equity that we tend to forget the reason is not making people feel good (though it does that), but the strength that comes from a plurality of voices. Nobody is right all the time, and that means an honest person is always learning; a diverse circle of friends enriches your life in ways you can be articulated because it will differ too wildly from person to person- you NEVER know what someone knows.

Synergy became a hot concept, then buzzword, and finally cliche, but people's power to achieve results greater than the sum of their parts remains. When everyone contributes freely, the result is a product exceeding all expectations.

It is not even so profound on a social level, or more accurately, the impact of small talk is measured in social fluidity and release of tension. Because just like there are selfish, materialistic reasons for diversity, inclusion, and equity, you can rationalize developing better social skills in a self-serving way, too. Stress is reduced when we are relaxed, and turning a stranger into a known entity does that. The brain also releases all sorts of hormones that aid socialization, dopamine and serotonin just two of the most famous.

Once you've made yourself presentable and found a group or person you would like to present yourself to, the only thing that remains is to make a move.

Just Do It

Bust a move. Break the ice. The slogans and expressions we use to motivate action over fear are almost endless. It seems like every other movie and series asks the viewer to believe the most important thing a person can do in life is conquering their fear. Considering the fact that most of us are our own worst enemy, and often the only thing holding us back is ourselves, this winds up being reasonably accurate.

Begin training yourself to push through negative self-talk, baseless assumptions, and biases: take action whenever you feel socially intrigued. In the case of socializing, the stakes are so low you really have nothing to lose. Even if you totally flub, as long as you laugh it off, the other person will too.

Even when making a move on a prospective partner, learning how to get shot down and not let it A) ruin your night and B) degrade your opinion of the person who declined is a great life lesson in itself.

Modern life lesson: be awesome and *keep your phone out of your hands*. Focus on the person you're speaking with, not letting yourself get distracted by your personal electronic device or anything else.

Ice Breaker

The expression "break the ice" is apt, as anyone who has felt a chilly social welcome and had it break into a warm reception will attest. A smile, eye contact, and maybe a firm but not crushing handshake can turn a simple hello into a solid connection. We went over clothes above, but in all honesty, the only thing you *need* to wear is a grin, at least. A kind greeting, open-ended questions about them, remembering their name, and a few salient details will make sure the next time you meet, will not only give them the warm fuzzy of being remembered but the extra thrill of having made an impression.

Memorize a few openers if you have a hard time thinking of things to say. We don't think about studying for an exam but think it's a betrayal of the human spirit to prepare conversations. There is nothing wrong with a bit of prep work as long as your motives are pure (no manipulation or exploitation). **Shared experiences** of any kind, especially pain or hardship and pleasures or joy (even minor ones), are always good conversation fodder and social bonding agents when experienced together. It needs to be out of your control, too. The lack of personal agency over topics of small talk is important unless you intend to do something about it (see Deep Talk further on).

As cliche as talking about the weather is, it is both shared and often unpleasant, so it fits these criteria nicely. Sports are the same: out of your hands, prone to go either way and are shared by a broad audience.

What is considered "small talk" will differ from group to group. Some folks are perfectly happy to throw around complex, even inflammatory topics right away, while others may never like to talk about contentious or overly complicated issues. "Read the room," and don't be afraid to back peddle or make a noticeable change of subject if you notice things taking a turn for the worst.

Keep It Going

Get the person talking about themselves. You can use the whole "nobody thinks about you the way you think about you" as an inverse, too. It is not egotism to enjoy answering questions of opinion and taste. Enough About Me, Let's Talk About You is classic for a reason, and if you notice yourself talking at length (not even about yourself but anything), stop and pass the focus to another.

It can be tempting to keep going once we get going because when we speak things aloud, we process them in a different section of our brain than when we think it, and then again when we hear our own words. This is "using someone as a sounding board," and while it is more of a one-way street than we typically like, it's a crucial component of conversation- as well as another "selfish" reason to be social.

Ask open-ended questions and **lean in** when they answer. In this case, you want to "lean in" in every sense of the term: body language is a crucial part of communication, so the non-verbal signal of leaning in is vital. It also means to pay extra attention, but more popularly, I've seen it applied to mean embracing something the world expects you to reject. For example, someone calls you a freak, but you lean into it and proudly proclaim whatever unique feature made the person try to bully you. On a day-to-day level, this means if you feel repulsion from someone, explore where those feelings come from and whether they are based on bias, preconception, or genuine threats.

Use cues on the person to determine what they might like to talk about. Beware of making a person feel stereotyped by making comments open-ended or exploratory. Never attempt to appear more knowledgeable than you are because no group likes pretenders in their midst.

You can change the subject if it goes someplace you don't like; be obvious if it's a point you'd like to make, or just keep making connections, mentioning related topics, and making tangents until it goes away. Conversations should be free and easy, but when all is said and done, there are just some things we don't want to discuss.

"Posers" are apparent in their desire to socialize over participating in the activity they pretend to practice and can annoy the in-group. This isn't to say there are not people there who are also socially motivated, but if you are not there for the activity but the people themselves, you have to ask yourself why? What about the group makes you want to know them but not participate in their interest? As long as you are following your bliss, there should be no issues because you'll already be surrounded by people doing what you love. Be honest and open, let a conversation flow naturally, and there should be no reason to put on a false front.

Break Away

You will eventually have to disengage from a conversation. Pressing commitments or flagging interest on your end can make a conversation feel like a cage. Knowing how to break away can be crucial, and doing so in a way that does not offend your audience is a great skill to learn.

If the gathering is sizable enough, you will be perfectly OK using the group itself as a pretext. "Oh, I just saw ____, and don't want to miss them" or "gosh, so many people I haven't seen in ages; let's get back to this later" are both excellent ways to say goodbye.

If you've been following good etiquette, your phone isn't out and in your hands during all this, so grabbing it and begging off to respond to an important text of call will be OK.

Needing to go to the bathroom, get food or drink is good too, though if you intend to avoid the person grabbing your attention again, you need to plan your move after, too. While I hate plotting or game playing in social exchanges and believe in stating your intent as much as possible, sometimes you have to make accommodations for the feelings of others.

At the end of the day, the only person you have to answer to is yourself.

Chapter 4: Step 4 - Make New Friends

In the first chapter, we talked about identifying what we wanted from our relationships and why. In this one, we put that to a practical application as we begin consciously assembling a circle of friends. Not the casual acquaintances that fate threw us together with but the like-minded folks we attract to ourselves based on mutual interest. Do not discount the power of shared experience. Know that people you went to school or work with are being acculturated to you as much as if you'd picked them out of a crowd. Choosing friends based on good conversations and healthy dynamics is always preferable to superficial similarities, so never be afraid to cross social boundaries.

Having begun to chat and then have a good time, you may want to get ahold of the other person again. This is where many casual run-ins fail to take root- neither side takes the intuitive to get contact info. After making initial contact, the second most challenging thing to do is **ask for their phone number, email address, or social media contact info**. With so many avenues of communication to choose from, even the most private individual should have a way you can get in touch.

"Take a Chance on Me"

Bullies are rare, mean people not nearly as brave in reality as they are online. The media has conditioned many of us to expect mania and stalking as a common occurrence. In fact, you can generally go your entire life without anyone becoming fixated on you to an unhealthy degree. It makes for good entertainment, so we see it all the time even, if not as many live it. Worse, reality television finds the most maladjusted groups to showcase, but many viewers see their own poor behavior on screen and feel validated.

The risk/reward ratio with meeting new people, making first contact, and letting friends deeper into your circle is always on the positive side: users, abusers, and the genuinely toxic are in the minority. Usually, we allow many small things to pile up until it reaches a breaking point. We also have to guard against letting pet peeves affect us too much.

That said, always be on guard against a con, casual theft, or other confidence-based crime; "fool me once shame on you, fool me twice shame on me" works fine. Forgive once but demand changes. Apologies that lack effort toward not repeating the behavior are empty. Professionals can treat even kleptomania: there is no place for any such behavior in friendships.

The more profound your relationship, the more you have to stand your ground. Looking for love means looking for someone to balance life with, and keeping oneself happy is hard enough. Friends do not usually require a lot of accommodation, the ease of interacting with someone only when we want to the entire point. Even long-term couples are encouraged to claim some space, a need for "me time," a universal constant.

"Just" Friendship

Let's face it: hookup culture is here to stay because it plays on human drives. It can be difficult, bordering on impossible, for some people to have a non-sexual friendship with someone to whom they are attracted. By the same token, many people fall into the habit of not interacting with the entire gender they are attracted to unless they are actively flirting. I cannot emphasize enough how important of a mental discipline it is to keep libido and casual friendships separate over the ordinary course of events. Modern culture has allowed for all sorts of freedom of love, and there is room in polite society for swingers, polyamory, and more. Still, you cannot flirt with everyone or otherwise sexualize every situation. State intent, be direct, and always polite; that means cheerfully moving on if your advances are declined.

The old advice used to be "no sex on the first date," but that doesn't seem to be the hindrance to a long-term relationship it once was. Changing attitudes toward sex mean a fair number of people just do not think it's a big deal. If your goal is monogamous intimacy or exclusive love, be sure you're upfront about it. Some people do not date friends, and some people won't hook up with strangers. Provided you do so in a polite way, even if you state your intent and the other person does not reciprocate, everyone likes to feel attractive, so very few will respond negatively. It is entirely possible to turn a friend into a lover, too, so while it is not a good reason to hang around all by itself, hearts can change.

There Is No "Friend Zone"

If you're *only* approaching someone because you want to have sex with them, and they are not interested, keep looking. I was always afraid of knocking someone up, creating a baby with someone I didn't love, so *at least* I tried to limit my dates to women I actually liked. This can be hard if the person "doesn't date friends" because right about the time I decided I'd like to date them, they decided they "didn't want to ruin our friendship!" Be forthright, know your heart and express your intentions early so you can avoid this kind of crossed opportunity.

Consider how terrible it feels to think you have a friend only to discover they were only ever interested in getting in your pants. It's a scenario women know all too often; an objectification that is anything but flattering: you're only valuable to the person as a piece of meat. Only pursue awesome people, and even if they turn you down, you'll be surrounded by people you love. Romantic or otherwise: aim for the group you want to associate with, be bold and break the ice by laughing at yourself. Don't assume they will reject you but just the opposite. In sales, it is called "assume the close," but in dating or even friendship, you simply call it confidence.

Hello, I Must Be Going

Things are going well, and all signs point to positive feelings: body language is inclined toward you, smiles and laughter are shared by all, and conversation is free-flowing and enjoyable. Unless it's a friend of a friend, and even then, taking this next step can still be essential to make sure they're your friend now too. You need to *hit them up for their digits*, though there are more communication options now than ever before.

- Well, this was fun; let's try and meet up again sometime.
- Dude. I haven't laughed this hard in ages; hit me up later.
- Crap, I have to go; let's do this again soon!

Any sort of declaration of enjoyment and a desire to contact them in the future will do, and putting it into your own words is a good idea. Mind their reaction, and offer something more public like Instagram or Twitter if they seem a little hesitant. Functionally the platform doesn't matter- just make sure you establish a point of contact.

You may even resort to the classic "how about we meet here, same spot, same time, next week?" or similar unplugged approach.

When to Call

Don't let the agony of "when to call" be some kind of test. Again and again, it is a point of drama in popular media, but you can curtail this little question by telling the person when they give you their info when you get in touch with them; better yet, ask. This isn't even a statement aimed at those seeking romance- making friends can feel just as weird.

"When are you free next?"
"I'll call you this weekend!"
"Can I call you tomorrow?"

They are all perfectly fine, but again, I want you to put these phrases into your own words as much as possible.

I like parties and gatherings as a pretext for getting to know specific people, as the crowd takes the burden off everyone, and the inclusion of mutual friends will help even further. Theme parties are only fun when everyone, or most people, are participating. For instance, throwing the links to easy, cheap costume ideas into a Halloween party invite will make sure everyone who wants to take part can. Masks, costumes, and dressing up are fun, so they can look very different depending on your social group. Formal is fun for some folks, as fashion eras, famous people, and even zombie/undead are all themes you can use year-round. Make an event of deciding on the theme, which can be almost as fun as the party itself.

Know "No"

Whatever your approach, taking no for an answer is the mark not only of a real gentleman but a mature human being in general. Accepting negative responses to requests without crying or begging is asked of children, but many adults fail this primary social developmental stage. Doubly crucial in your romantic advances, accept the rejection and move on; maintain friendly, even mild flirtation, but only if they continue to smile and incline toward you. If you have already established a little familiarity with them, you have made your interest known and *might* have planted a seed. However, as I mentioned before, being friends with someone *only* because you want to sleep with them after being denied is rude if not plain wrong.

It's OK to be sexually attracted to friends, but it can't be the only reason you're there.

Be a Friend

When passing people close enough to encroach on their personal space, smile, nod and if it's not too out of place, say "good morning" or whatever is appropriate. Often just a grin and nod will do, but the more whoever you see have in common, the chattier you can get right off the bat. Over time this *will* develop into more genuine smiles, prolonged greetings, and eventual introductions; when you run into these persons in other places, the reaction will be even better.

Walking dogs, minding children, and watching the same show are only the most common examples, with any communal activity as good of a shared experience as any. The more unique the incident, the better: an exclusively shared memory is even more bonding than one shared by many. Helping someone when they are in a jam is a perfect way to demonstrate what kind of friend you are; just be sure your help is desired.

Help or Hinder?

When someone is struggling in public, they will cast their eyes about if looking for help. In general, I always ask **"how can I help"** before I begin any aid because a situation can look deceiving, or pride can make people touchy about getting help, too. The adage "the road to hell is paved with good intentions" can be negated *only* if you stop and ask first.

If a friendship is all you helping them or being helped, you're on maintain balance. The caregiver is a personality trait just as much as "chatty" or "analytical." Still, you cannot fall into the habit of letting people grow dependent on you, or you grow co-dependent on them.

Chapter 5: Step 5 - Keep Friends

We always think of "taking things to the next level" in terms of romantic relationships, but there are levels of platonic friendship, too. Taking an acquaintance to friendship and a friendship to a more profound point still is something that ordinarily happens all by itself, but some of us might need a little nudge.

Generally speaking, we share ourselves with people we are closer to, interact with them at a greater frequency, and are generally more generous, too. Time, talking, and small favors all amount to a kind of currency; our personal time is as essential to many of us as money itself. When we invest effort into a friendship, and it fails to thrive, it can feel almost as heartbreaking as being rejected by a lover, but just like seeking a long-term relationship, we cannot let a setback become a stopping point.

The favor bank is funny; as should be obvious, when we request a small thing from someone, we feel better about the person who helped us. However, brain scans have revealed we, the helper, like the person who asked the favor more, too! As long as it is not too big and does not become routine, there is a two-way bond when we help each other out in small ways.

However, the so-called Favor Bank is a bank, so make sure you observe the balance. All take and no give make both parties disrespect the other. Do not let yourself become a doormat, and at the same time, remember to reciprocate when it comes time for you to give a little of yourself.

Do a few of the following throughout the year, invite different groups of friends for larger gatherings, or keep it small with a few select persons.

Host

- Dinner Parties
- Sports Viewing
- Holidays
- Birthdays
- Anniversaries
- Theme Party

Offer to use your space; it will be a huge relief if the other person is worried about the impact. Giving your home to use is a risk, though, so don't do so unless you trust most of the guests. Nothing ventured, nothing gained, though, so throw the doors wide and let in the masses.

Get In Touch

It is all too easy to let friends drift away. Once enough time has gone by, the span itself becomes a perceived obstacle, and even more, time goes by. It is never too late to contact an old friend, and it is almost a guarantee that the other party will be happy to hear from you. More times than not, the simple forces of life moving forward cause people to lose touch, and in the case of kindred spirits, it can feel like no time has gone by at all. **Reach out** and touch base; you'll be glad you did.

Throw a reunion party if it's been so long. Mix new and old contacts and see who meets up. High school reunions can be fun- or absolute torture: find your old clique and make your own.

The modern age made it pretty easy to look up old friends, and social media allows people to remain in contact with those you may never have been able to. Don't let the updates and shares fool you, though, and make sure you meet up in meat-space if you value the friendship at all; what we share on those platforms is usually a pale sliver of our whole selves.

Shake the Family Tree

Genetic tests have put people in touch with each other who didn't even know they existed. Email addresses and phone numbers are usually included with relations who have also used the service. You don't even have to go to the extreme of tagging your genome. Just begin calling family and seeing who knows who. Researching ancestors is fun, and doing so with family is so enriching. Overall, unless you have had to cut toxic people out of your life, don't let petty or even major conflicts permanently estrange your family.

Occasionally, friends or family demonstrate an inability to function in a healthy and meaningful way. Maintaining healthy boundaries is key to any long-term friendship, and if the other person demands much and gives little, it might be time to sever ties. We will get into the specifics of identifying and dealing with negative traits further on.

"Besties"

Almost invariably, you will find a few friends with whom you really hit it off and spend most of your socializing with them. Or you can form or join a small club or group only to find that socializing takes priority. Many bridge clubs and reading groups wind up being for sitting around talking first and the point of focus a distant second. In these kinds of groups, be sure to remember balance and equity.

When eating out in large groups, split the bill. If not everyone was drinking alcohol, separate the cost of drinks so non-drinkers don't get soaked.

Let everyone have a turn picking the location or activity.

Extend invitations to people you would like to see regardless of your expectation of them saying yes. Everyone wants to be invited, whether they are busy, tired, or slightly agoraphobic.

Mix it up; if you always gather at the same place, try another. Favorite restaurants are great but don't be afraid to try new things. Same with homes: one person might enjoy hosting or have a more comfortable home, but circulating to each other's places will keep conversations fresh and give one another a deeper appreciation of each other's lives.

You form a pack and can socialize in tandem, working as a unit. In such tight-knit bunches

Make New Friends but Keep the Old

Some are silver, but the others are gold. I always thought that was an unkind adage, but you realize how true it is as time goes on. It might be based on shared belief or just uncanny clicking, but there are acquaintances and not-so-good-of-friends in our lives, too. Unless you have definite reasons to exclude them, don't forget to include these folks in your medium or larger gatherings. You never know when someone's hidden corners will reveal themselves, and if you never give people a chance to surprise you, they never will.

Forged In Fire or Bonded Over Time

Deep, meaningful friendships either flare to life spontaneously, meeting the other person like finding a long-lost sibling or another half of yourself, but usually, it takes time or pressure. Like diamonds and metamorphic rock, the composition of your social connections changes when you go through an ordeal or spend long enough time together. The "ordeal" could be as bland as work or school, though the more mortal your peril, the more profound a bond is possible.

Of course, too terrible, and the sight of the other person can become a trigger! Army buddies are either fast friends or avoided; how trauma affects someone varies significantly from person to person.

Those seeking to grow closer through this kind of activity should look toward back-country camping or organized sports. Playing competitively or pitting yourself against nature will bring out the person's true self. Not that we deceive or hide, just that different aspects of our personalities come out when we are pushed to our limits. You can get away with the more low-key activities, but then it's a matter of time instead of sweat.

Quick Tips
- Sustaining interactions; enriching or stimulating
- Frequent but not too much

- Resist drifting apart; host parties, little gatherings, or just lunch
- Resolve conflicts as soon as you can; push through temporary discomfort
- Expect change; people are not static, we don't stay the same
- Honesty and integrity in all your dealings, especially friendship
- Support; ask how you can encourage and aid them
- Respect boundaries and take no for an answer

It can be challenging to articulate the nuances that go into forging solid bonds. Still, the points do a pretty good job contextualizing something that isn't usually conscious thought. Even if we grew up well adjusted, raised by emotionally intelligent people, and learned this stuff intuitively, it can be a good idea to go over the particulars and check ourselves for hang-ups, bad habits, or blind spots. We all know by now that nobody is right all the time, but the flip side is we must admit when we are sometimes wrong, too.

Be a Friend

It really cannot be said enough: if you want stronger ties, be a stronger friend. Show up; say "yes"; be agreeable. All the while, make sure you're not over-extending, giving too much, or too little. Sometimes, it becomes necessary to confront problem behavior or otherwise resolve a conflict in the course of a friendship. Many of us practice avoidance and ignore or turn from difficult situations. It is the mark of mature, strong personalities to grapple with the unpleasant as soon as it comes up, instead of shoving it down.

It is easy to laugh and have a good time, but true friends are the ones who stick around through thick and thin.

Chapter 6: Step 6 - Go Deep

It's easy to be friends and generous with your time and resources when the times are good. It is easy to socialize and have fun while never scratching the surface. Over time, if you don't go deep at some point, you will either drift apart or blow apart. Life is unpredictable, and if your whole relationship is based on predictability, at some point, life is going to come crashing into the room.

Some of our friends might be struggling. Sometimes you may feel inclined to help. It is crucial you announce your intent and then ask how you can help rather than just begin interfering. As mentioned, it may be foolish pride, or you may misunderstand the situation and make it worse. As much as we'd like to, sometimes we can't save someone from themselves, and all we can do is step back, cut ownership of their problems and let the chips fall where they may.

Observe, Consider and Decide

Not everyone is strong in the "personal reflection" department and what seems like an apparent conflict or eventual problem to you is not something they have even considered. Sometimes all you have to do is call attention to something. Other times the person will consider your words and decide they don't see it as a problem. You Can Lead a

Horse to Water but Can't Make Them Drink is true enough, though a good friend will at least try to point out how thirsty you are.

Stretching the metaphor as far as it'll go, if you take the horse to the spring and *try* to make them drink, at best they'll sputter, choke and gag and at worst, you'll drown them and give them an aversion to water. Decoding the now tangled meaning there, you might just end up alienating the person or making them averse to seeking help in the future. An open hand, guiding by example and with gentle encouragement, will always work better than brow-beating or dragging them.

OK, now that you have decided to meddle in someone's life, you have decisions to make.

Run Toward Danger

If you know a conversation will be difficult, you should have it as soon as possible. Procrastination is not a time management issue but an emotional one, so get a hold of your fear and have the talk you need to have. Often, we are far more worked up over a topic than the person is, and our tension and stress are wasted. Other times the person responds poorly, but as long as you use "I statements" and address the concepts surrounding the issue and not make it sound like a personal attack, you should be in the clear.

Examples include:

"I feel you might be wrong about this."

"I feel your drinking is affecting your life in negative ways."

"I feel you may not be taking care of yourself."

Deconstruction

When it comes time to get down to brass tacks, try to talk about ideas and concepts. Think about the motivations behind the behavior instead of dwelling on the behavior itself.

If something someone does is bothering you, make sure you understand why before you launch into what they can do to change. Maybe the problem is you.

If they cannot change something, or it's a minor characteristic trait that is not harming anyone, you might just have to work on changing your relationship to it.

Complaining

When we hear someone complain, it can sound like a cry for help. It may be a plea for aid, but we hear it as simple venting. When we see a friend is freaking out about something, we can ask ourselves, or even them, simple questions.

Are you processing right now or looking for suggestions?

Let the person know you hear they're upset and want to help while at the same time acknowledging that they may not be in an action-oriented mood and are just expressing themselves. Unsolicited advice usually doesn't go over very well, and your intent to help comes across as condescending or judge-y. This is also gentle encouragement that there is an "action stage," as so many people get hung up on their complaints and anger, they wind up nursing the wound instead of healing it.

Philosophy, Religion, and Spirituality

Sharing the same outlook will make these kinds of difficult conversations a little easier because using a shared vocabulary in a mutually agreed-upon belief system will make sure you don't have to stop and define your terms all the time. Even if you do not share their cosmology, knowing what they believe will make sure you will be able to couch your discussion in words they understand.

As much as possible, make sure the conversation remains grounded in life. Faith is all fine and well, but agonizing over perceived spiritual crisis should always be balanced against real-life. Usually, if someone is feeling like the forces of good and evil themselves are at work in their life, there's a reason for it. Seek out reactions, see if you can determine a cause-effect relationship triggering the problem, and treat that.

Existential Dread

Rooted in the word "existence," existential is just a word that means problems relating to being a living being on Earth. Usually out of our control and universal, existential crises grip all of us at some time or another. Our ability to roll with it will be determined by our ability to let go of things we have no control over.

Aging, children growing up, the classic death and taxes stuff can all pile up in our psyche if we are not careful, the so-called "emotional baggage" a real problem in some people. Make sure you're not lugging any around, the definition being cumbersome thoughts and behaviors resulting from reactions against past slights. Let go of the past but focus on the here and now; you cannot undo mistakes of the past, but you can do everything in your power to make sure you aren't repeating mistakes.

Enrich, Explore and Enliven

Not everyone likes to have deep talks, but we all need to sometimes. While some folks whip out big ideas and begin asking your thoughts about God right away, others open up quite a bit slowly, if they do at all. There's nothing extraordinary about profound thoughts if you don't share them, and there are aspects of ourselves we do not really get in touch with unless we discuss them. When we share the parts of ourselves we barely acknowledge, we come to realize just how similar we are and how silly it is to be shy about sharing.

The statement "we have more in common than different" is intrinsic. It goes from the surface to the core. The more we talk about our fears, pains, and dread secrets, the more we realize everyone has the same or similar feelings. At the same time, we might discover that what we've been living under the pall of is entirely benign. Having worked ourselves up into a froth over a thing, to find it's easily resolvable or even all in our mind is a relief greater than you can imagine.

Still, those deep dark agonies are real at times, and there is no silver bullet for the inner demon that plagues you. In those cases, talking about it with yet more people is far better than bottling it up or limiting council to just one individual. The greater my dilemma, the more voices I like to get involved. While not everyone will have the same experiences, if you have gotten into the habit of looking at forces and influences instead of things and people, you should be able to gain insight from almost any source.

Break It Down

Money troubles are by far the most common. Using currency concerns as an example: it is past time to make a formal budget. If you don't know what the sum total, even roughly, of all your monthly expenses are, then tally them up and keep the figure handy. Can you downgrade, cancel or readjust spending to free up some cash flow? How much are you eating out; research menu planning and less expensive options. Is your career wasting your time? Make an improved resume, polish up some old skills, acquire new ones, and look at more lucrative job options.

Love troubles can be circled around and studied, too. There are currents in relationships almost like the currency of economics, and if you are not savvy to non-verbal and encoded messages, you can be caught off guard. Better yet, do not rely on analyzing and guesses; intuition is a terrible way to navigate a complex topic like intimacy. Talk about feelings and discuss your past because you carry your early loving relationships with you through life more than any other aspect of life. I keep hearing the expression Love Language, and it is true that not everyone will express love the same way. Talk about your upbringing; talk about your first loves and losses.

Ultimately, the goal of deep talks is to make sure no topic is off-limits. Trust is built, earned, and if it is lost, some people will never give it back.

Chapter 7: Step 7 - Build Strong Relationships

One should earn trust. Respect is a given up to a point, but genuine esteem and honor are built up over time. Growing stronger bonds is like nurturing a garden more than it is like constructing something- I cannot say "do a, b and c, and the result will be x" any more than you can scatter seeds and expect them all to become mature plants. We can do everything possible to foster goodwill and gain a closer relationship with someone, but that person is always an independent agent and may drift or even disappear. "If you love something, set it free, and if it loves you back, it will return; if it doesn't, it was never meant to be" is of unknown origin but holds true.

Making sure you do everything you can to encourage closeness (without going total stalker) is the final lesson. You have friends; you have the tools to maintain friendships and explore more profound aspects of life. What can we do to strengthen our solid connections into unbreakable bonds?

- Let it happen; time and patience
- Boundaries; respect theirs, maintain yours
- Get to know the individual; honor the individual
- Be as good as your word; hold them accountable
- Respond to feedback; give as good as you get

- Mindful reflective responses, not reactions or knee-jerk opinions

Having covered all the topics earlier, boundaries and accountability may be the only ones we haven't discussed in depth. Give people space, and be sure you encourage consistency. What that means in a practical way is a little more complex but pretty easy to understand, as they are human universals.

Go, See and Do

Hobnobbing, chit chat, and chewing the fat; all sounds pretty passive. Do not let all your interactions with friends and loved ones be sedentary- do things together. It is almost like young people know this instinctually: kids are constantly exploring the world together, teens go cruisin' (I think?), and as adults, we can make friendships into lasting, deep kinships by dancing, camping, or taking classes; even just going to new restaurants and into new shops achieve the same result.

We often look for shared experiences when we form friendships, and lacking those but still enjoying one another's company, the best thing you can do is go out and *make* some. The decision itself can be illuminating, as you the two of or group try to come up with a shared activity, peoples interests and aversions come to the fore. Watch for a dominant personality. Every group seems to have one, so see that they do not abuse their power. For it is power, minor and subjective though it be, and some people must always be in control at all times.

It may not even matter to the group if the gatherings are low-key, low-commitment; who cares if Jane always has to get her way or John calls all the shots when nobody else has a strong opinion, and everyone can leave when they want? These people should still be called out if not challenged, so at least you know if they are aware of their "my way or the highway" manner. More times than not, selfishness is innocent myopic thinking, and unconscious egotism is usually the result of birth order or routine indulgence.

Take a Back Seat

If the part before describes you, take your hands off the reins and let others in the group call the shots. Even if it's just conversational, if you see yourself sucking all the air out of a conversation, pause, apologize and consciously let someone else hold the floor. Sometimes circles of friends will simply put someone in the de facto leadership position, and decisions default to this person. Make sure it's because they are well researched or at least well-reasoned, because more times than not, it is simply the most charismatic or talkative one who decides.

Acceptance

Most of all, we have to take our friends at face value; this doesn't mean we judge them superficially, but it does mean we have to take them at their word. We can see things in people they do not possess; our insistence that we are right and they are wrong about *themselves* can be a wedge that drives you apart. This extends to self-improvement and personal development, too, I'm afraid; as much as we love someone, it is not our place to tell them what to do. Live the example, offer help and support but know that you cannot live a person's life of them.

When we take the time to think about someone else's point of view, we enrich our understanding of the person and our ability to communicate with them.

Humans' only constant is diversity; not even twins are guaranteed to be the same.

Space and Boundaries

We all need "me" time. To varying degrees that change over time, everyone needs to be alone and enjoy a little unfettered freedom. The practical application of respecting "no" is sometimes letting the person be by themselves. Even the most gregarious social butterfly needs to be still and turn within sometimes. If you disagree, if you always feel an unrelenting urge to be with people all the time no matter what, revisit chapter one's Date Yourself lesson. Even if you don't think you need it, humans do require even just a little personal time.

Without a little Me Time, it can be easy to skip over deeper issues with superficial chatter or otherwise distract yourself with other tasks and topics. It is harder to run from ourselves when we are alone and we are forced to confront ourselves. If we have a healthy relationship with the self, this type of self-care is terrific. However, getting to this point can take practice, so if you find yourself at loose ends when by yourself, see if you can reflect on a source. Having tough talks with your inner self is just as important as any other friend.

Accountability

We always want smooth sailing, and making waves can seem like avoidable friction, but time and life honors nothing, and the occupational conflict can arise. Broken promises and canceled plans have an accumulative effect, so mind you are keeping goals and sticking to your word. Trust is not something to squander. When we extend a friendship, we are usually trusting the person to reach back. At its most basic, mutual accord requires someone do what they say.

It really cannot be overstated: **if someone steals from you, lies, or manipulates you, leave them**. You may be included to forgive someone once, but make it clear and in no uncertain terms- "fool me twice, shame on you" means the same thing as "Never be the same fool twice ."We learn from our mistakes, or we never grow; if we continue to repeat the same error, again and again, take a step back-analyze your feelings around the issue and why you might be hitting your head against a dead end.

If They Hit You, They Do Not Love You

While an abuser may insist they love you, if their love language is abusive in any way, you are encouraged to run, not walk, away as fast as you can. It is a personal problem on their end, and until they address it in a meaningful, lasting way, you owe it to yourself to stay away. Love involves a *little* personal sacrifice as some of your free time is dedicated to another, but anyone that would ask you to suffer under their love is wrong.

If you are in an abusive relationship, know that I emphasized "abuse of all kinds," to include emotional and psychological abuse. We look for bruises or tears when we look for violence against each other, but manipulation and exploitation do not always look so obvious. Nobody gets to be right all the time, nor does anyone get to skate through life never saying apologizing. **Apologies have to be accompanied by an effort to correct what was wrong** or an apparent effort not to offend again. Saying "sorry" but continuing to offend is empty and a further offense.

Unhealthy love languages and an upbringing full of conflict can make healthy relationships seem out of reach, but you have to know that most of us are survivors of damage. We can break even the unhealthiest cycles with patience and a willingness to change. Bad habits can be inner or outer, in the form of negative self-talk, nervous ticks, or addiction. It is difficult, if not impossible, to maintain strong friendships when you are struggling with behavior that feels out of your control.

Beyond Self Care: Self-Help

Compulsion, addiction, and dependency are all well understood psychological phenomena. Break vicious cycles by studying the thought-feeling-action cycle around it, stepping in the middle of that crucial circle of habit, and rerouting the pattern into a new one. Never easy, always a long-term process, making lasting personal change is a little easier if you can replace problem behavior with a healthy one. Breaking bad habits fails more often when we make no effort to replace one activity with another.

We all know that, no, jogging is probably *not* going to feel as good as, say, smoking; at least not a first. But jogging releases dopamine and other pleasure chemicals, and the same are true for all exercises and many activities.

Nurture Your Nature

As a final word on building better bonds, play to your strengths as you play to theirs. Being alone together is totally a thing, as introvert/introvert pairs know pretty well.

In general, circulating out in the world with a new friend is an excellent way to encourage rapid growth, as travel is enriching in general and you can do so together. Respect some folks who are the opposite and find the new experiences too overwhelming to socialize through; I invite those folks to confront those discomforts and seek help if the problem is insurmountable.

Seeking a professional's advice if not help if you are unable to help yourself is the last lesson in this guide. Sometimes a problem has a chemical root, and medication is the only way to feel normal. Other issues are too deeply buried or entrenched to resolve without a third party, so never be afraid of seeking aid.

Conclusion

Never forget that friendship is a two-way street; give as good as you get- be sure it's not a one-way street, and everything should grow well. For the most part, a social connection should be stimulating and enjoyable. If you find yourself avoiding a person or situation, explore your feelings and if you have to, write it out. You may find the problems you have with other people are problems you have with yourself. Other conflicts arise organically from fundamental, meaningful disagreements. Whether or not you decide to let it go and move on or drop the person from your life and move on is up to you. But life does move on, and it takes effort and persistence to maintain lasting friendships.

Take a stand or will not stand for it?

Modern life has created artificial depth to minor issues, and more so than ever before, complex problems are being over-simplified and glossed over. Should politics play a role in your personal life? Religion has always been a prime motivator for social dynamics, so goodness knows there have always been wedge issues. But the longer we allow our list of "deal breakers" to grow, the smaller our friend circle is and the more narrow our point-of-view grows.

Keep your horizons as wide as possible and your circle of friends as diverse as you can tolerate. Even if you think all that unity and peace stuff is BS, the potential for growth and new, better ideas grows exponentially the move voices we allow at the table. Reach out, reach back, just reach out and make contact.

Plumb your past and look up old friends while sending feelers out to find new ones. Plants send taproots out into the soil around them to find fresh nutrients and moisture sources. Do that, but with your life. Explore conversationally. Do not assume the quiet person doesn't want to talk but their body language; "resting mean face" is often an illusion, so risk a friendly, polite greeting in passing.

Be You; Stay True

Nobody owes you a smile, though, so don't demand a positive reaction. At the same time, never feel obligated to respond to friendly advanced with anything more than polite indifference if you're not interested in reciprocating. Pleasers should learn they do not have to win everyone over, and loners should open up a little let in a few people. Balance and moderation with your interpersonal communications make sure you are not burning yourself out or bottling yourself up.

You can stay true to yourself while taking on aspects of those around you. "Mirroring" is when we start talking and acting like the people we wish to bond with, and it is primarily unconscious. Make sure the social groups you are attracted to are healthy ones, as often we can be attracted to particular cultural or even fashion traits, but the only people in our areas doing them can be selfish or rude. Be the change you want to see in the universe and "do you," boldly go and do as you like; nobody owns a style or clique, and you are always free to reinvent yourself.

Make today the day you start talking more (or less!) and confidently hold forth on topics you are interested in, making it conceptual or idea-based, if not the thing itself. When we hold ourselves back from socializing, we rob not only ourselves of missed opportunists, but the world around us suffers from our lack of contribution.

Book 3: Persuasion

7 Easy Steps to Master Influence Skills, Psychology of Manipulation, Convincing People & Negotiation Skills

Lawrence Finnegan

Introduction

Welcome to "Persuasion". Exerting your will; Getting others to change their mind. As innocent as flipping someone's opinion or potentially life-changing as seduction, of all the communication skills an individual can develop, Persuasion is the most powerful and, therefore, most mistrusted. It is easy to see why learning how to influence people's thoughts, and even behavior is looked at with suspicion: we are not talking about simply asserting ourselves but pulling others around to your position. We will learn how to leave the realm of merely remaining true to ourselves and cross the threshold to persuading our fellow humans to change their minds. Salespeople, priests, teachers, counselors, and so-many others know persuasion skills; now you will too.

Despite how persuasive individuals hold many helpers and beneficial roles, the reputation of those skilled in this art is not good. Too many selfish people have pushed too many credulous or trusting folks into actions they would never have done without being coerced; such is the power you now hold in your hands. This may be the only guide you follow which comes with a warning: over-application of the skills presented here may result in driving people away if you unrelentingly try to change the mind of everyone around you! Like so much in life, moderation is vital, and one must be extra judicious with something so strong.

Persuasion is not manipulation; manipulation forces someone to do something Against Their Own Interests. Sooner or later, the target realizes what happened, and if they are not happy with the results, it will be on you.

Utilizing effective powers of persuasion ranges from subtle to crusading. Drawing people to your conclusion with suggestion and passive guidance or actively challenging objections while leading the conversation both have their time and place. Every situation will demand a different approach, and learning how to pivot that approach on the spot is powerful. We go over the seeming paradox of remaining nimble by defining an unmovable core. While we work on changing other people's minds, we must always be on guard that the people we are changing benefit from our proposals.

Again and again, I will urge you, to use these skills constructively. You can think about being genuine and honest selfishly AND altruistically if you need to: nothing will pit people against you like the feeling they have been manipulated. Using people is counterproductive, and in all cases, you must weigh what you are getting from the persuasion against what the other person does.

Whenever you are asked to take a moral stand, we back it up with logical, cause-and-effect relationships. You do not have to take my word for anything but support even the most emotional-sounding declarations with facts and proven research-- just as you will once we are through. Far from harping on you or beating a dead horse, we make sure we do not drift into troublesome waters by regularly checking ourselves. Because the motivational speakers, life coaches, and cultural vanguards we all know and follow use some of the same skill sets as con artists, connivers, and charlatans. Like a superhero, you must decide to use your powers for good instead of evil. Evil, in this case, is defined as using someone against their own interests, lying, and insidious manipulation.

Enough with the admonishments. It is time to sit up straight, get ready for some practical exercises and take the first step toward a more persuasive personality.

Let's get started!

Chapter 1: Step 1 - Be Confident

When we begin to talk about persuasion and what it takes to bring another around to your point of view, we have to start with confidence. If you have not convinced yourself, you should not expect to persuade others. While significant career changes and essential skills should never be lied about, "fake it till you make it" absolutely applies if you are not feeling confident. A talent like any other, persuasion must be practiced to develop it. Fear not; the homework is easy or at least laid out simply. In the sections further on, we will break Confidence down into its elemental parts, the near-mystic quality we used to ascribe to charisma now fully understood.

You don't have to be a shrinking violet if you do not want to be; the wallflower can bloom. Even the most socially awkward, fumbling word klutz can, with a bit of practice and motivated self-interest, get to conversational competency and beyond to the interpersonal communication Master Class of Persuasive Speaking. All of which is based on having at least a little confidence.

Take a Stand

There's no denying that confidence is catchy. Behavioral study after behavioral study has demonstrated that crowds are more susceptible to passionate speakers than knowledgeable ones. You do not need to look too far in this modern age or history to see humanity is swayed by strident, emotional appeals and passionately delivered rhetoric as much as well-reasoned, logical statements. The power of a charismatic individual to move entire populations is well documented, which is why it is so important to check your motivations. I made the distinction between Persuasion and Manipulation in the introduction because it is so important not to use your skills to the detriment of those around you.

Even if you lack moral fiber or any collectivist mentality, nobody likes being used. You risk undermining everything you are working towards once you begin using people against their interests. It is practical: you *will* encounter these people again, and while folks are pretty forgiving, once someone feels you have wronged them, you may as well consider that bridge burned. However, we are a social beast and tend to default to abdicating personal responsibility-- there is a part of us psychologically loves to make someone else think for us.

The willingness of people to put decisions, both trivial and significant, into the hands of others is nothing short of profound. Everyone gets at least a little of their thoughts and feelings from others. It is the brain's way of conserving energy: we trust another to do the logic and reasoning, so we do not have to. As far as it goes, sometimes you simply have to have to. Nobody knows everything, and seeking expertise is often necessary.

Fake It 'Till You Make It

Until you actually feel confident, it is permissible to act like it. Indeed, just like nobody is right all the time, nobody is going to feel confident all the time. As long as you prepare, you can at least feel sure of your material, and practice will make sure you are not stumbling over the words for the first time. You never want to 'fake' fundamental skills or fabricate experience, but displaying more confidence than you feel is an ability worth sharpening. Suppose you fake your way into a role whose functions you cannot fulfill. In that case, you harm not only your prospects but the entire organization while affecting confidence, and then suddenly revealing your hesitation will humanize you. I've said it a few times now, so here is How to Fake It.

Monitor your breathing, posture, and eye contact: confidence looks relaxed, with normal breathing and casual body language. Your chin is up and back straight, but you are not looking down your nose or appearing stiff. Meet others with a steady gaze and no fumbling language. Slow your delivery, if you have to, so you can remove "uh," "um," and "ah" from your speaking voice. Those kinds of hesitating non-words rob you of credibility and make you sound unsure.

Except using those kinds of halting, unformed sounds can give the listener the impression you are choosing your words carefully. When you are replying, these hesitancy sounds can work toward establishing you as an active listener. In a reply or when talking about a new concept, they can indicate you are considering, actively thinking about your response instead of just waiting for your turn to speak.

A little loose, even casual language can work for you in professional settings if applied in moderation.

Business Casual

Used sparingly a little bit of casual language, even slang, in the middle of an otherwise professional discussion can add emphasis or lighten the mood just as much as telling a joke outright. As an ice breaker, nothing beats an unexpected moment of familiarity. This technique actually plays on the expression "familiarity breeds contempt," although in this case, the "contempt" is ironic and simply rough language. As paradoxical as it sounds, such a casual attitude signals having held a position for a long time, being thoroughly familiar with it, or otherwise as a term of endearment. However, loose language as a positive does not have universal appeal, as some parties find any lapse into informal speech in professional settings irritating. Indeed, some people take a straight-laced, buttoned-up attitude home with them, which is a reason to continually be monitoring feedback, analyzing how your actions are received.

You do not want to overdo it, but with a very modest application, throwing in the occasional common term instead of technical, or even an expletive if the company is right, can give your position strength. However, colloquial language only works judiciously and in the right company.

'trash talk' is most common in some sports and competitive groups. However, anyone unfamiliar with the world of competitive events and games may take it personally, so beware when employing this in new groups. It is usually best to start with the Absurd or Trivial when attempting to engage in lighthearted trash talk for the first time or with a new person. Observe a few simple rules at first if you do not know the basics: some people take it too far or take it too personally, so if you have not picked up these unspoken rules by exposure, here is a rough guide to start you out.

What You Can Trash On

- Things under their control: haircut, clothes, music, personal style
- Impossible or absurd: "Yo momma" jokes, Do you have a broken leg?
- Nearly anything goes with someone whose boundaries you know.

As counterintuitive as it seems, this course language brings people closer. As it progresses, you usually get more and more raunchy, extreme, and bizarre. Again, however, not everyone participates in this almost ritualistic slamming of one another. If you start in on someone who does not understand the jocular nature of the exchange, it will have the opposite effect– you are going to drive a wedge when you intend to build a bridge. It is almost tempting to say, "just don't initiate it," but throwing a ridiculous or humorous jab at someone can be a great ice-breaker, assuming they are receptive to that kind of humor.

Knowledge Is Power

You don't want to be a 'blowhard' and suck all the air out of a conversation as you demonstrate expertise when discussing a topic, but you want to have researched and investigated, so you are ready to clarify any points. If possible, explore all sides of anything you intend to persuade anybody. Even if you do not use the knowledge you have gained, the assurance in your voice and general vocabulary will add weight to your words. We have already discussed how it is often not what you say but how you say it; having a solid foundation of research gives you gravitas. When a word is unfamiliar, be sure to look up the correct pronunciation.

Earned or Assumed

Swagger can either be faked or the result of experience. Literal "swagger" is not professional, of course, and even in many social circles strutting around is not likely to go over too well. However, carrying yourself confidently and speaking in no uncertain terms has great weight. Initially, uncertainty is OK, even encouraged. Nobody is right all the time, so someone who is always sure of themselves is almost certainly full of themselves. Acknowledge your limits, own mistakes, and admit when you are wrong. When it comes time to attempt pulling another person around to your point-of-view, though, you have to be as adamant as possible.

Acting and passion both grant people the ability to project confidence, but nothing beats experience and actual ability. There is a reason army recruiters are almost always vets or why school principals without classroom experience flounder against those who do. Experience with the subject you are wielding is only one part of it. There is respect given to people who have actually gone through what they are presenting, saying nothing of the mental bearing that comes with practical, hands-on experience. If you find yourself in the position of needing to convince people towards an action you have not taken yourself, you begin at an almost impossible disadvantage. Get in there and do it. "If it's good for the goose, it's good for the gander" is an idiom reminding you not to try selling something you are not willing to buy, metaphorically or literally.

If you find yourself in a place where you are attempting to motivate people towards an action you have not taken yourself, it may be time to reassess your motivation. Confidence is great unless you are confidently marching off a cliff.

It can be challenging to find occasions to practice confidence. Usually, it is a matter of seizing the opportunities as they present themselves unless you have situations in life you routinely avoid. Look for interactions in your life that make you nervous (or however you express the opposite of confidence) and tackle it head-on.

- Carry yourself with conviction: posture, stride, and energy
- Speak your intent clearly: be direct, state your need
- Unwavering eyes: stop just short of staring them down

Chapter 2: Step 2 - Work on Delivery

Know your audience as much as possible. The expression Read the Room is crucial advice when you are trying to persuade and convince. If you have the chance, choose a suitable format to deliver your message. Younger demographics do not engage with media the same way older ones do. I've had teenagers laugh at the idea of us 'old timers' using Facebook– though when pressed, they admit to having one "just to talk to grandma." Make sure you are right, or at the very least research and analyze all sides to make sure not only that you are correct but can answer common questions about why you may be wrong, too.

Reading the room is the same as monitoring feedback. Unless you can take real-time notes from the audience, we have to vary our words, tone, and stance by non-verbal cues alone. While it may seem strange, checking in with your persuasion target can be a great tool to use when driving home a point. Make use of the fact that people love to talk about themselves. "What do you think about all of this?" or "Why don't you tell me what you feel about x?" can give you all the insight you need to begin bridging the gap between your interests and theirs.

Happy

Almost without exception, you need to be positively beaming when you take the position of changing minds. It is not good enough to simply grin if you really need to sway. Even the sourest of us are attracted to joy, and positive emotions will attract all but the most hardened cynic to happiness. More than playing on the instinctual role humor plays in social bonding, it makes people wonder just why you are so happy. However, overplay this attitude and risk being seen as simple or even feeble-minded. So be sure you demonstrate what makes you so happy as you create or increase a radiant smile.

People have varying degrees of comfort with high levels of happiness, with many taking the attitude that the current state of the world leaves little to be happy about! Maybe nothing so existential, but remember that there are some who you quite simply cannot impress with a cheerful disposition. Always read the room, monitor the reaction of your words, and most of all, you must be ready to dial it back or crank it up accordingly; freezing up and blazing forward regardless is a common mistake. Taking time, practicing, and observing your audience will always pay off.

Multimedia

Maybe words are not even what you want to use. Smartphones and streaming media have shortened the average attention span considerably, so making short, you might consider related videos or podcasts. Look for opportunities to use these tools, and deploy them instead of a text or live message whenever possible. These can be boring, so if you go the route of multimedia production, make sure you use post-production software to sweeten the sound, add graphics, and edit out distracting gaffs. While intimidating, modern software is designed with novice users in mind, making most common changes intuitive or discoverable with a quick internet search. You may think of or discover even more modes of communication that work even more effectively.

While being "correct" is, unfortunately, not as important as it once was, being well-researched and familiar with all sides of a debate will only ever help your cause. Even if facts do not sway the person, the attitude you carry when well-studied is unmistakable. Reading common arguments against what you stand for makes it easier to defend your position when attacked. Many people simply challenge new ideas by reflex, so just because you get naysayers in the beginning is no indication the person is genuinely contrary- they may just be making sure you have considered all angles.

Fast or Slow Tempo

Fast-Talking Salesman is a hated cliche for a reason. While you never want to fall into the temptation of deceiving someone, a hurried delivery can be impactful. Some folks will never trust you if you talk too fast, while others will doubt your cognitive faculties when you speak too slow. The largely unconscious social phenomena known as "mirroring" essentially take care of this without knowing. The brain is hardwired to imitate what it wants to align itself with: you will naturally talk faster with people who do the same and slow down when confronted with someone using a decreased cadence.

Resist the temptation to judge one way or another. Some people are wired for speed. Their hummingbird-like metabolism does not indicate their competency or overall abilities. Likewise, some people who speak slowly and with rudimentary or straightforward vocabulary can be heinously intelligent, not everyone valuing word choice the same. Give people a chance, do not resort to bias, and in general leave as much as possible open to discovery. Make no assumptions, but state your needs clearly. People will only surprise you if you give them a chance.

Reflect and Consider

When you are in the home stretch, you have stated your case, and the person sees things your way, it is important to restate their objections. Remind them you have thought about the alternatives, their point-of-view is valid, but your position considers aspects they did not even consider. By acknowledging that two people of identical backgrounds and education can be confronted with identical facts and come to differing conclusions, you assuage their ego while comforting their minds. Prove your dedication to the truth by identifying your audience's own.

Demographics

How old is the group you are addressing, on average? What is the prevailing gender? While "class" is no longer the term used, from what socioeconomic background do they come? The term *class* has become obsolete because it is generally accepted that ability, aptitude and overall potential have less to do with where you are from and how much money you and your family make as it does the opportunities you've had and your individual drive. Not relying on bias and prejudice is a cautionary statement, not a humanitarian one: you underestimate (or overestimate) people at your peril. While we can and should speak to groups, we must never mistake the forest for the tree; we can describe a population but never forget their inherent individuality.

Heated rhetoric from news and media might make you think twice about making any kind of generalities. Still, in reality, humans categorize and label as a matter of brain structure: our minds will impose a pattern on something without order as it attempts to understand it. Knowing that generalizing and pigeonholing are inevitable, one can get in front of it, anticipate it, and even take advantage of it. Appeal to "group think," make playful Us-Vs-Them declarations to inspire teamwork, and otherwise remember the positive side of clannish cliques. Stronger social bonds, wider networks, and more diverse ideas are only the start. Protecting yourself against bias, prejudice, and plain old incorrect assumptions is crucial to maintaining truth, so be sure you do not fall into the trap of offending those in a group who do not identify with it.

In practice, this is as simple as adding qualifiers.

"So many," "a lot of y'all out there," "*some* kinds of *x*," and similar statements are a great way to not get into hot water when straying toward the general. As long as you belong to the demographic you are referencing, there is no limit to the stereotypes and generalizations you can use. As an outsider in a new group, and you had better tread lightly, being liberal with the exceptions IF you decide to stray into their subculture at all. Some cliques are exceptionally touchy about the language "outsiders" use, though reporters and bloggers will note these kinds of hot-button words or issues as long as you are doing your research.

Do Not Pander

The death of credibility, the downfall of well-intentioned persuaders everywhere, is condescension. Every demographic is made of individuals, and people are touchy. If someone thinks they are being talked down to, they are likely to shut down and ignore everything you say if they don't just walk away. Nobody likes being treated like an idiot. Masters in their field must always guard against coming across as condescending or rude when explaining the subject of their expertise to a layperson. Always assume the best of the people you address, never fail to be polite and considerate in your words and actions, and you will have gone further to establish your credibility than if you had written a book on the subject.

Adjust

Some people labor under the delusion that confidence means blazing forward regardless, staying the course no matter the opposition, and never changing tact once the destination is set. When you are being responsive, however, this is not the case. An adept speaker, capable of swaying entire crowds, watches the audience and modulates their delivery accordingly.

Is the audience restless and not paying attention? Establish a point-of-focus with a visual or handout. If everyone is nervous, tell a joke, or simply acknowledge the tension, ice-breakers exist for this reason. Sometimes bringing awareness to something is all it takes to change it. No one laughing? Change your humor. Too much laughing? Rein it in. You are not "reading the room" if you are not aware of how you are being received and adjusting accordingly.

Chapter 3: Step 3 - Find Mutual Benefit

By absolutely no surprise, people will find themselves moved to follow your lead when there is something in it for them. We tend to think of 'selfishness' as a negative trait, and it certainly is toxic when taken to an unhealthy degree. However, a little ego is necessary in this world, outside of monasteries and nunneries. It can be tempting to dig in your heels and unrelentingly pursue your every goal and plan, but finding strength in unity will beat out a selfish individual every time.

Appealing to humanity's never-ending drive to socialize is powerful, and getting the other party to Yes can often be as easy as learning how people define their terms. Get people talking about themselves, motivations, and passions. Keep them going, let them open up, and soon enough, you will find common ground. We all like being a part of something. Being In makes us feel good, and in today's social climate of isolation and exclusion, it can be even more rewarding to seek out and join a clique of some kind.

It is possible to turn a No around into a Yes without being manipulative and cajoling, as long as your objective has merit for the affected party. If you find yourself unable to think of a reason why a person would *want* to change their mind, you may be leading them astray. I have said it once, and I will repeat it-- even if you are OK bending the truth and using people, you cannot change someone's mind with lies and deceit and expect it to stick. Motivating people to act against their best interests is the domain of cult leaders and fascists, so mind your motivations well. Indeed, consensus-building and the formation of coalitions are often done subtly by people more interested in pushing their agenda than stroking their ego.

Compromise Is Strength

While we talked about not budging, you must understand the power of a compromised idea. When everyone has had input, when the group is confident all its members' interests are taken into account, you can be assured the results will last longer than if you are following an individual's vision. Indeed, democracy itself is founded on the idea of strength in acting with group consensus in mind. Follow one person too long and, even if they were up to the challenge of sole leadership, it is chaos and disarray once they are gone. When the entire group makes a decision, a lone dissenter cannot so easily overturn everything. When everyone puts their heads together, ideas can be generated which are greater than the sum of their parts.

In the economy of ideas, no one is allowed a monopoly. Again we refer to the old saying Nobody Is Right All the Time. In this case, as we remember to tune in when brainstorming, make creative decisions with as many people as possible. Let folks participate, meet their eyes and nod enthusiastically when they deliver an idea, and do everything short of cheerleading if it means getting people to share their thoughts. The reluctance to share creative output is legendary, so do not forget to schedule some ice-breaking or introductory exercises to loosen up strangers. If you can get a group comfortable enough to share, the results are always surprising and far more substantial than if a single mind made all the shots.

Still, sometimes there is only one way forward, and no compromise is possible. Either the decision is out of your hands, and you are little more than a messenger, or you have superior information; whatever the case, there are times you just have to "carry the ball forward." When you have no wiggle room, there are still a few tools at your disposal when persuading.

Change Nothing but the Words

Assuming you need to "stick to your guns" and no aspect of whatever it is you are trying to assert is changeable, you can alter the way you are saying something without being disingenuous. Saying the same thing in different words is another factor research and collecting other viewpoints helps: you have to know how to phrase things differently. Understanding as many synonyms, a few good metaphors (and pointing out where the similarities break down), and as much about the background of origins of your position will help. You circle, bridge one topic to another, and otherwise make sure when you begin to guide the conversation, it is by reasonable steps and not broad leaps.

Preface what you say when you rephrase something with a call-back to what they said. Relate as much of what you say toward any objections or misgivings they have relayed to you, and they will feel validated, even if you act contrary to their wishes. Many times, we just want to make sure our voices are heard. Adults seldom expect to get their way all the time, so compromise is expected. We all protect our interests, though, so knowing what your audience simply will not budge on is fundamental. Knowing a person's most solid, unmovable beliefs will give you something to leverage; find a way to incorporate that core value, and the individual is more likely to follow. If the person does not have a strong opinion on the matter in question, give them one.

Framing

Knowing *why* someone made a decision can loosen stubborn holdouts. As long as the reason makes sense, most of us understand the power of compromise or are willing to bend. Giving context of any kind can make all the difference, with trust and honesty required to make this argument. By referencing the Big Picture and the result you are hoping to achieve, it is often possible to bring someone around based on nothing more than a shared destination. Appealing to the bigger picture is why doing your homework and researching what you will persuade is essential. Plugging what you want into a grander plan takes the focus off yourself, making the change you desire to look more like a change expected by a grander scheme.

Once you have broken what you want down into its core concepts, you might find you have been fighting for the wrong aspect, wasting time on secondary or tertiary objectives. If your goals are lofty and have enough imagination, seeing the broader perspective becomes easy. A chance to consider all the angles, giving ground on small matters can maneuver you into a better position to succeed on bigger ones.

The Power of Capitulation

We talked about identifying the other person's objective so we can cater to it, but what about your own? Have you deconstructed what you are doing and considered the endgame? If you can locate what you desire out of a situation, you can occasionally discover you do not need to "win" at all. The idiom Lose the Battle but Win the War should ring true because this is not a battle, and 'losses' in this case do not amount to much. In one of the chapters further on, we detail how winning a small victory can snowball into more substantial wins. We aid this immeasurably when we allow for small 'wins' on the other side.

Give ground if it is not essential. Ego often gets in the way of real progress, so if allowing the other party agency over an aspect of your pitch that doesn't affect the overall outcome, let those affected call a few of the shots. Owing to people just wanting their voice heard, if possible, let other people have their say. Giving ground and letting people call some shots becomes more critical the better you get at persuasion; if folks notice you grabbing the wheel all the time, they will want a chance to drive. Small gives now set the stage for more significant asks later, so remain flexible in the planning stages so you have more control over the final product.

Reciprocity

Foster interdependence between your audience. The result of compromise is you Both Get What You Want. Don't get distracted by the small stuff, make sure you do not lose sight of your objective, and never give up something you need for something you want. If you have a hard time juggling details and losing track of the big picture, try journaling. If writing isn't your thing, mind maps are fine. Get your ideas out on paper or out of your head if you are using a computer or other medium, so you can thoroughly explore all aspects of what you are trying to achieve.

The more flexibility your objective has, the easier it will be to get other people on board.

Realizing that not all objectives will be dynamic enough to allow for this sort of give-and-take makes looking for areas you can bend all the more critical. You should consider the other person's choices as collateral or currency. You can risk the Illusion of Choice if you want, but that gambit is easy to see through over the long run. An individual who is most often easy-breezy, go-with-the-flow but all the sudden puts their foot down and declares a strong opinion has a much greater chance of getting their way than the individual who always gets their way trying to get it again.

Locate those aspects in your life that you often raise opinions about or otherwise control the direction of, and let go of control if possible. Obviously, in professional settings, or other areas of expertise, this is impossible but learn to enjoy the ride if you are usually the pilot. Weighing in on the side of nobody being right all of the time is the idea that nobody should call all of the shots all of the time. On a national level, such didactic command is fascism, and on a more personal scale, it is just being bossy.

Grounded

You will not have to worry about coming across as bossy when using higher powers as your guide. I don't mean religion and God, though finding yourself surrounded by the devout certainly gives you a predetermined set of motivations, but science and logic. Appeal to cause-and-effect, observable, verifiable facts, and your arguments will make themselves. Sometimes, this is literal. There are occasions you can tell someone about a new idea, have them research it themselves, then come back and admit you were right. But this is only possible if you hew to logic and reason yourself.

Chapter 4: Step 4 - Favor Logic & Reason

Make sure you are confident for a good reason: *are* you right? Is your position of personal interest, or is there anything in it for others? If you have established yourself as honest and fair, people will trust your opinion more often. The more information and data inform your decision, the less subjective the result and the wider the potential application. Having researched new material, can you realign your position to encompass more viewpoints? Recall that an agenda woven from the ideas of others is resilient and adapt with assurance.

Informing your opinions with facts means when it is time to change your mind, more people change with you. Staying current is not a matter of popularity but maintaining credibility: you were right before, people might expect you to be right again. As we will see further on, there is an autocatalytic component to being right, which is to say it is self-feeding. Once you are known to have answers, correct, well-researched, or reasoned solutions, folks will be coming to you for decision-making help more often. Be careful: too adept at this ability, and you have friends dumping all their stressors on you.

With so much information out there, it can be hard to separate the wheat from the chaff; separating the useless from the kernels of truth is a lesson unto itself. Bewildering as the Information Age may be, knowing what to believe is easy once you know how to vet your sources.

Reliable Sources

If you went through any college or had to cite sources in high school, then a little of what I am relating will be familiar: if you could not use the resource on an academic paper, you should not use it, period. Opinion pieces and experimental science are fine, as long as you talk about feelings and theoretical concepts. Even in that last sentence, I must qualify what I mean– the "theory of gravity" is not the same kind of Theory as your theory of what happened to your car keys. A "theory" is technically verified by experiments and is verifiable instead of the common usage, which implies uncertainty. We have to watch out for these changes in meaning as we look at ideas more closely.

When parsing our arguments for veracity, testing them for truth or application, it is essential to look at the counter-examples or views against even more than those that underscore your point. We *have* to challenge our beliefs rigorously, doubly-so those we are attempting to push on other people. Look at the criticisms twice, as **cognitive bias** creeps into even the most disciplined of minds and falling into 'confirmation bias' is all too human: we want to believe things that confirm what we already "know." Cognitive Bias is the term for a group of logical fallacies into which our mind routinely falls. The brain only accounts for 3% of our total mass but consumes 20% of our caloric energy! To conserve power, you're thinking makes short-cuts, usually by categorizing and grouping things– it is easier to think of "Them," for instance, than it is to think of "Bob, Nguyen, Susan, Joe, Fred, Juan, Daphne, and George."

The topic of how our evolutionary biology and psychological framing can undermine our success is far too broad to analyze here, but entering Cognitive Bias into a search engine will give you many excellent examples. Since it is endemic to the human experience, knowing you are doing it and taking steps to free your arguments of unsubstantiated information will put you at an advantage. Cognitive Bias is so hardwired into our neurons that some techniques are employed to persuade people to take advantage of them. Manipulation and coercion are more accessible to spot and confront than someone playing on your very brain chemistry. Don't let the brain's remarkable ability to work against itself trip you up. Since your influence over an individual will flip instantly the moment they mistrust you, we must hold onto your integrity and attempt to operate from a position of truth and fact whenever possible. Trust is hard to earn and nearly impossible to get back once lost.

When no research exists to support your position, look for trends, similar concepts, and what history has to say about it. Your educated guess can become quite accurate with enough familiarity with comparable systems. We live in an age of novelty and discovery, but those new frontiers are almost all under the surface, or so epoch-shattering we won't even notice it until it is in the past.

Trust

Again, even if you do not care about morality or being liked, coming from a position of research and data will give you far more power than playing on emotions and other forms of exploitation. If people find themselves agreeing to something they would never usually say Yes to and see you at the helm, you may have lost their faith entirely. Humans are quick to condemn and slow to forgive, defense mechanisms making a single act of betrayal wash out one hundred positive interactions. We have to make sure and remain above-board as much as possible and work toward being straightforward and honest in all our dealings. Still, "to err is human," and as long as you can demonstrate your ignorance or show actual change, it is possible to regain esteem in people's eyes. Should you find yourself on the positive side of a 'mended fence,' you had better guard against repeating the behavior: few people are willing to forgive twice.

All notions of right and wrong aside, exploiting, controlling, and any kind of coercion of those around you is, at best, a short-term gain. If you persist and lead a team through deceptive or disingenuous methods, you might have a good or even above-average result. Still, you will never enjoy the kind of synergy that comes from the free exchange of ideas, inter-group equity, and otherwise honoring the individual's perspective.

Credibility

Dependability goes a long way. As I have said before, Nobody Is Right All the Time, and as long as you only change your mind when confronted with superior data, you should be able to retain the confidence of others. If you find yourself being the know-it-all, step back and make sure you are correct. Never apologize for being right, but you do not want to rub folk's noses in it or overplay your hand. The master trivial knowledge can be a valuable resource on any team, but if you insert factoids into every conversation, you are squandering your asset: people will tune you out.

Acknowledge the negatives but focus on positive outcomes. Own it when your position is attacked, and their criticism is valid. "Yes, you are right about that" is powerful when the other person is expecting a rebuttal or denial. Don't turn around and point out the flaws in the opposition's side just yet, but state the fact that no plan is perfect and outline how your drawbacks are minimal. Honest assessments of one's position, including its flaws, give you an edge over people unable to admit any fault. This evenhandedness is where research and study pay off, too: you may find yourself in the wrong and abandon your desire to change anyone to your side.

There is a tendency in some people to never **admit fault**. Whether it is true narcissism or just lazy thinking, once it is noticed that you never say Sorry and never take responsivity for your actions, your credibility is gone, and you have to work twice as hard to sway people. Look for "sorry," "I was wrong," and similar statements in your exchanges, and keep your ears open for it from others, too. Cognitive Bias or cumbersome ego, some people are simply self-centered as a default status but still like to think they are generous and fair-minded. When considering every possible angle, guard against spending too much time pondering.

Overthink

You can analyze too much, throw too much processing power at a problem and overheat. At the end of the day, when confronted with seemingly equal choices, we can take a leap of faith. Decision Paralysis occurs when you are frozen in a dilemma, with too many options or nothing to make one stand out from the others. When we find ourselves in a situation like that, it is perfectly OK to shoot from the hip, make a quick decision and go with what 'feels' right. When we rely on our instincts too much, when we guess when we should be thinking things through, we get ourselves into trouble.

Intuition Is Not a Guess

Assuming you have been using reliable sources, your intuition should be somewhat accurate. Occasionally the unconscious mind is working on a solution and just sort of pops out an answer, seemingly from nowhere. It is the result of dreams, unconscious thought, and it is increasingly becoming apparent information from the brain cells in your gut. Far from being random or meaningless, sometimes those spontaneous answers can be 100% accurate. Knowing the difference between a real gem of intuition and a random, free association or non-sequitur is virtually impossible, so be sure to exercise a healthy degree of skepticism toward such results.

Life Lessons

Learn for its own sake. Embrace a spirit of discovery and curiosity.

Never accept "I don't know" when you have an online computer in your pocket. They say that every child is a natural scientist because kids seldom take things at face value and run experiments all the time. We lose our sense of wonder as we mature, but it is something some of us never let go of, and you can relearn. Don't *just* stop to smell the roses, but examine the micro-structure of their stamen and how it resembles the bee it wants to attract *as* you smell it.

There is a reason for everything. Nature has been refining her designs for millions of years, so at least in the natural world, you can seek and find answers on almost everything. Mysteries and discoveries are just below the surface, and many of the solutions we think are correct today will be disproven tomorrow. We are at our strongest when we are open to those changes.

What doesn't bend breaks, but we should remain rigidly unmoving on facts until we get better data. To "agree to disagree" on good foods, favorite movies, or interior paint color is excellent. But the Earth is round, the climate is warming up, and the minimum wage in America is too low; there are facts, figures, and dozens of corroborating sources to support those statements, yet surprisingly vast swaths of the population would argue those points.

When confronted with unmoving wills, you might have to make a tactical withdrawal when chipping away at stubborn attitudes and strong feelings. Far from a retreat, if you know someone is not budging on a big issue, you might be able to turn the tide by starting small.

Chapter 5: Step 5 - Find Some "Yes"

Start small to go big. Look for minor, hopefully, related things to agree on first. A person who agrees with you once is far more likely to have a desire to continue to do so. The power accord is why there is nothing small about small talk, and allowing yourself to drift off-topic and let their attention wander onto something else can sometimes help your cause. As we refer to it here, the whole point of small talk is to get the person nodding their head, making agreements no matter how seemingly trivial. It is not something that is ever taught, much less articulated. Still, when we engage in these kinds of light, introductory or fleeting exchanges, we look more for validation and social bonding than anything else.

If you launch right into your pitch straight away and then try to go back and get small victories if they rebuff you, it will be transparently obvious what you are trying to do. The power of small talk is why most salesman training courses advise you to start with almost anything other than your objective when chatting with someone for the first time. When the person is in a sales position, this can be hollow and not as effective, but as long as you are not in a role where they will be expecting a persuasion, you should chat someone up pretty quickly.

Small Talk

You can start a conversation with anything, but be sure to steal a glance and take some cues from the individual you attempt to persuade. Know your demographic information, follow trends and styles within the group you are trying to sway. It is impossible to stay on top of all of these, and of course, individuals will always vary, so keeping things as general as possible at first is usually recommended. Unless there is a tell-tale sign of what the person is interested in talking about, we can start with the weather, sports, or any other common openers like aspects unique to the location, irritation with authority figures, and gossip. Social trends have been veering away from gossip, and you should never say things you would not want the subject to hear, so observe discretion when talking about people who are not present.

Again, people on guard against manipulation will usually call you out and demand to know what your objective is, so be ready to own up to what you are doing and, most importantly: why. As long as you have e a defensible position ("I was trying to help!"), you should be OK, if not now, tarnished by having meddled in their life.

Ultimately, you just want to get the person to open up and begin giving you information on their own. We are not talking about sensitive or essential information but whatever the individual wants to talk about. Indeed, whatever they bring up is important to them, and in any case, sharing generates feelings of social bonding, which is a sociologist's word for kindling friendship.

And you always want to make your friends happy.

Suppose you are in a position where it is obvious you will attempt some sort of pitch. In that case, starting with something completely unrelated and personable can be incredibly disarming. Skip the related content, disregard your desired goal and just dig into the exchange. Make these excursions off track briefly if time is limited or just let the person carry the conversation away; as long as there is a next time, you can cash in this social currency later.

Gift of Gab Deconstructed

Stay casual, keep it in their wheelhouse, and if at all possible, find at least one concept to align on. A topic of interest can be as broad as you can manage and still appeal to the individual's tastes. Some people *love* talking deep, their enjoyment of conceptual and idea-laden conversation so great they hate 'small talk;' to them, deep, philosophical discussions *are* small talk. Most folks are perfectly comfortable with either, or some get pretty uncomfortable when you try to pull them into the deep end. Feel people out; if "how about this weather" feels too cliche, you can sometimes get the conversation started with even more superficial, less specific openers. A polite and sincere "Hi, nice to meet you," delivered with warm body language can go far, as can passive comments on what brought you together, be it the topic of a conference or simple transit stop.

If you can determine whether the person you attempt to sway is more collectivist or independent, that is huge. Give the independent spirit room to customize and as much wiggle room as possible, and give the group-thinker instructions, guidance, and precedence. Both chaff under the burden of the other, so it is a crucial split to observe. Spiritual and Secular ideals are pretty strong signifiers, too, and with as strong of polarizing applications: an atheist might bristle at religious content. Some theologically inclined folks do not take some scientific explanations very well. The more intrinsic and long-held a belief is, the harder it will be to change but easier to leverage. You may not be able to tell a creationist that they are their own worst enemy because we evolved for hunting and gathering but live in cities, but you might try, "that's the way God made us in the Garden of Eden."

Open-ended Openers

Not everyone likes their job or is otherwise not defined by it. So asking "what do you do for a living?" can tell you nothing about the person, and if the job is stressful, it can take them right out of the moment. Asking "So what have you been doing with yourself?" or "What kind of music do you listen to?" leaves the door open for them to take the thread where they want. Leaving your introductory messaging open-ended and personal lets the person know you are available on any topic and not just interested in talking about your interests alone.

Agree With Valid Complaints

Let people object and even change the topic while you remain aware enough to bridge the conversation back to your objective. You will lose all credibility you have earned if you insist on being right all the time. Since nothing is perfect, admitting a weakness implies the strength of self-awareness or acknowledging all influencing factors.

Not a Battle

Everything in the United States gets turned into a fight. We love our martial metaphors from the War on Drugs to the War on Poverty. Suppose you are going to persuade as many people as possible. In that case, however, we have to rid ourselves of the mentality that every conflict or disagreement must have a winner and a loser. It starts with never wanting to give ground on anything and is dictatorial. Sometimes we simply get addicted to winning and begin seizing the lead reflexively in every situation. As soon as you free yourself from the need to control everything, you gain the power to control things you need to.

Some groups have gone so far as to issue new, less authoritarian leadership titles and insist on calling themselves Organizers, Facilitators, or Focalizers. While the power of words is considerable, changing your title will not fool anyone into listening to you anymore or less. Everything we are outlining in this guide will determine your audience's receptivity, as actions most definitely speak louder than words. Your words and efforts make a boss an organizer, not the honorifics themselves. Lead by example, and you will find people lining up behind you.

Build accord. Seek consensus. Regularly check in with the other party and make sure your reaction to what they tell you is measured and neutral: people will stop opening up if you react negatively to everything they tell you.

Keep Your Cool

As you navigate the conversational waters ahead, you ideally look to go from Yes to Yes. We talked about the dangers of being seen as pandering, which is why maintaining a genuine spirit of curiosity and wonder comes in very handy: people will be used to you exploring new ideas and asking a lot of questions. The truth is there is strength in either side of dichotomies, and a fusion of two or more winds up stronger than one alone. As social creatures, we are definitely stronger together, though the unrelenting diversity of our psychology makes absolute conformity stifling. As we get closer to 'sealing the deal,' whether it is an actual sale or just an opinion that is important to you, we have to remain positive, on track, and easy-going.

As soon as we grow heated or even over-excited, we risk losing the person's empathy but show too little vim and vigor, and you will appear dull or disinterested. Let the tangents come as they naturally do, then, if possible, direct the flow back in the direction you want through indirect connections as much as you can. Some folks stay on the topic pretty easily, so shifting the focus of tangents back on track is not always needed. By maintaining a casual attitude, we convey to the listener that as far as we are concerned, what we are talking about is a foregone conclusion; we are confident in our position. Remember how easily people mistake confidence with competence and move the thread where you want it.

Chapter 6: Step 6 - Be Patient and Persistent

Directly related to the Small Wins concept is taking your time and never losing sight of the goal. Carefully shepherd the conversation, guiding the language until they see things your way or you are shut down in no uncertain terms. Sometimes the way forward is sideways, and going around is what it takes to bring you where you need to be. In some cases, you cannot take no for an answer, and dogged determination is the only chance you have. Humans naturally tend to dig in their heels and stubbornly resist even beneficial advice if they feel personally attacked, which is why keeping things light, easy and agreeable is essential. As long as you have observed all the tactics outlined earlier, you might be surprised by the person you are attempting to sway bringing the desired topic back up themselves. Another facet of small talk is our ability to engage in it while also thinking of other things.

Most of all, in this lesson, we need to pay attention to how our message is going over as we monitor and adjust our phrasing and body language accordingly. This point of the conversation is the home-stretch, and if your persuasion has been based on lies or is otherwise exploitative, then this is house-of-cards time, and any wrong move will send you back to square one. In truth, being caught out manipulating someone can send you back further than square one, down into mistrust. Having been called out as such can be insurmountable, and if possible, you had better move on and find a group you do not need to deceive to win over. Knowing when you are even close to that stage is crucial, so slow down and watch your audience.

Stay Tuned In

Empathize but stay on target. Observe the distinction between Sympathy and Empathy as long as we are on the topic. When you sympathize with someone, you take part or all of their emotions in yourself. Seeing someone cry makes you tear up or even begin crying yourself, or the classic infectious laughter that gets everyone going whether they thought it was funny or not. On the other hand, empathy is when you know the person's emotional state and understand why they feel the way they do, but you are not affected. As quickly as some people get swept away with strong feelings, others have a very tight lid on it and seldom lose their cool. Remaining aware of your words' effect on the other person will give you all the cues you need to make all the right moves.

Receptivity is why making and keeping eye contact is essential, though there is an often-overlooked side-channel to eye contact, and that's peripheral vision. With a bit of practice, you can encompass the whole of their body into your view, not only their eyes and face. Posture, what they are doing with their hands, and general level of tension can all be detected, so make sure and consider the whole picture and not focus only on the face. Still, the face is a huge part of communication, so you will be OK if that is all you have. Look for how they hold their jaw, the forehead, and neck: all are places we carry and display stress.

Get good at this skill, and you may even be able to detect feelings the person is not even aware they are processing. The unconscious mind can wrestle with things just like your train of thought, and hunched posture, drawn or pinched face, and clenched hands can all indicate the person is grappling with existential problems. Don't let the word intimidate you: Existential means Stemming from Existence so that we can get hung up on practically any fact of life. Noting such tiny details is usually viewed as compassion. However, if the individual is private, victimized, or doesn't like people getting too close, your observation of these things might be seen as invasive or rude.

We expect loved ones to be aware of these kinds of subtle signals, so when someone we just met starts to bring up our feelings and ask us about our thoughts, it is usually quite endearing. Distractions and other people can make maintaining an emotional connection difficult; we must tune in, though, or curving a tangent back to the task will be all but impossible.

Steer the Conversation

Ask open-ended, even rhetorical questions. Inquire about the other person because few people do not like talking about themselves at least a little bit. Be sure you remember the highlights of what they tell you so you can call back to it later. Whether you get them speaking under their own steam or you wind up talking more than listening, make sure the conversation thread is woven into your design as much as possible. As in most things, a modest measured approach to conversational control is critical. At the same time, don't make broad leaps or assume the listener will make the same connections you did. It's all about laying breadcrumbs, placing a trail of logical inferences for the person to follow. You set the stage with questions whose answers you already know, tempered with the understanding that they might come to a different result. Sticking to logic and facts will make this infinitely more manageable than appealing to somebody's feelings, which vary significantly from person to person and even from day to day.

As much as possible, use what you have learned about the person to make sure everything you are saying is relevant or at least interesting. The saying goes, "you can lead a horse to water, but you can't make it drink," so the best you can do is try and make it recognize it is thirsty. Torturing this metaphor even further, you should be aiming your initial search for horses that are thirsty or otherwise need water. Once you cross over into the realm of convincing this figurative horse they need water when they do not, you have breached the threshold into manipulation and coercion.

What often begins as well-intentioned mentoring can become telling everyone what to do. Even the most patient teacher wears thin and starts snapping at people, and we must remember to take into account terrible days, unique moods, and unusual psychologies. There is no Silver Bullet for percussion, and two people will not be moved the same way. Take the time to learn a person's desires and drives, and you can even turn a minor setback into a significant gain.

Losses Into Gains

We spoke earlier on the Power of Yes, but we cannot forget how admitting flaws in our position gives us strength through credibility and repeatability. When we are being honest with ourselves and our research, including conversations with others, we are bound to find ourselves in the wrong at some point. Admitting we are wrong can be one of the hardest things some people do, while others have a bad habit of apologizing and taking responsibility for things that are not their fault. Stay consistent and accurate so others know what to expect of you. Develop a reputation for this sort of ego-free consideration, and you might find people proactively seeking you out for your opinions. Once this happens, most of the work is done for you; just say well-informed and committed to fairness.

Next, in the spirit of It Is Not What You Say, But How You Say It, we look at practical, explicit advice on achieving a demeanor to match your nature. As promised, in the last chapter of this guide, we explore charisma itself, strip away the mystic and misunderstood, leaving behind a core set of lessons anyone can practice to put a little extra shine in your presence.

Chapter 7: Step 7 - Be Amazing

As much as we would like to live in a meritocracy, we are led by the lucky, privileged and charismatic as often as not. As unfair as it seems, just as essential as being right is being well received. "Flattery will get you everywhere" is meant to be a humorous inversion of Flattery Will Get You Nowhere. Still, we all know how favorites are played. Oligarchy and insider advantages do not even have to be ill-intentioned or conspiratorial: it is often simply a matter of being in the right place at the right time, when the powers that be need a particular skill and, hey, there you are. Since Who You Know is going to matter at least as much as What You Know, learning how to turn up the congeniality and charm the socks off of people will be a valuable tool. Even if friendship and social bonding aren't your ultimate objective, there is nothing quite like shared opinions to grease the skids.

As this guide progresses, more aphorisms and idioms have cropped up. Cliches and turns-of-phrase all come from folk wisdom and are familiar to everyone yet nonetheless engender a certain amount of ownership. Most people like hearing things come out of other people's mouths that they have in their head, and throwing around common expressions is just the start. Making sure you stay up-to-date on changes and trends works out to this benefit, too; echoing the thoughts of people you don't know is a powerful thing. Sometimes you have to go in cold, and that's when general rules of presentation and charisma come into play. Friendly confidence coupled with helpful, well-thought-out advice will take you far. Avoid the pitfall of offering unsolicited advice, however.

Likable And Influential

How exactly do we turn up personal magnetism? Having chosen a passionate topic and researched it from all sides, how do we give our presentation, formal address, or casual conversation the final shine it needs to break through the last few barriers? By adhering to some basic grooming standards, ensuring that our non-verbal cues are on point, and taking to No for an answer.

Appearance

Appearance is a little less critical than it used to be, but people will ignore you if you do not tend to yourself a little bit. Historical standards of personal upkeep were impossibly high by design; the need for servants and handmaids to even get dressed was a sign of wealth and status. Even the last century saw entire sections of the population that would not even look at you unless you conformed to their expectations. While a high level of conformity and displays of wealth are no longer seen as positives, the lingering effect of centuries of status symbol clothing and accouterments linger. Fresh, wrinkle-free clothes and groomed, clean skin and hair are essential if most folks are going to take you seriously.

Non-verbal

Non-verbal signals must be in line, too. Angle your body toward the person you address and lean toward them a little. Crossed arms make you look closed off or guarded, and leaning or slouching gives the impression of disinterest. Arch your eyebrows, slightly part your lips, or touch their shoulder or hand in surprise or agreement when they make a salient point. These mannerisms are usually automatic when the feeling is genuine, so be careful when you decide you want to force it.

Eye Contact

Eye contact creates intimacy and makes the person know they are the center of your attention. Many people report difficulty making or maintaining eye contact, so if this describes you, it is paramount that you work on it. The warmth and familiarity created by prolonged eye contact are just too powerful a social lubricant to avoid discomfort.

Make sure a smile accompanies **your gaze**, or you risk coming off as intense or demanding. Work a chuckle or **laugh** into your delivery, too. Sociologists have noted that across all cultures, people laugh more than half the time at statements made without the intention of humor. We laugh to signal agreement, surprise, and trust. Once you begin looking for it, the amount of non-humor laughing is quite remarkable, considering we associate it with jokes and wit.

Call Backs

Call Backs to what the other person has said earlier will cement your reputation as an active listener. Even better than finding common ground is creating common ground, and referencing the person's thoughts later in the conversion will take your influence over them to a whole other level. It can also be extraordinary when you hear your words come out of someone's mouth, and if an idea is half-baked or only loosely held on to, hearing it come out of someone else's mouth may be all it takes to make them see the error in it.

Practice

Practice whenever you get the chance. If you are genuinely afflicted with social anxiety disorder, proven therapies can get you over it. Record yourself and pay it back; review yourself as if you were a stranger. Re-record; this time, try to sound better. Work on the tone, cadence, and content of your words. You might feel conspicuous at first, and it might make you feel silly the first few times, but there is nothing like media capture and review to analyze your speaking skills. You can change anything, even if you laugh if you want to.

Prerecord

If you have the opportunity at all, you owe it to yourself to make a video or audio recording of your message so that you can deliver a perfect form. There is just no getting around the fact that your delivery will vastly improve if you have the time and take the effort to polish the message until it shines. In this increasingly digitally interconnected world, where asynchronous communication and video conferences are part of The New Normal, you can take advantage of people's growing comfort with multimedia messages and position yourself in the best possible light.

Light can be literal, as good lighting is one of the things you want to look out for when reading your shot. Fluorescent lights make you look washed out and even greenish, and indirect lighting casts hard shadows that can be distracting. Make sure that nothing is distracting in the frame of the camera, as well as eliminate as much background noise as possible.

If you are sending a prerecorded message, take as much time as you need to make it perfect. You have the luxury of post-production, as well, so there is no reason to send out anything other than your very best. There are dozens if not hundreds of freely available and inexpensive entry-level videos and editing suites out there, and I highly recommend you familiarize yourself with at least a few of them. If you are to make the most of your canned messages, tinker, adjust and re-record until you are happy. Since we tend to be our own worst critics, if you can get your final product to a place you like, the recipients will almost certainly love it.

Just like your face-to-face encounters, keep things loose and casual unless the situation calls for formality. Nobody will want to watch your video if it's boring so remember to use big gestures, slightly elevated emotions, and lots of eye contact– That is, looking directly into the camera lens as you are recording and not the screen. Quite unlike your face-to-face exchanges, you can get a second 3rd and 4th chance to make a first impression here.

In all of these versions, try different cadences and tones of voice, mix up the order of your content and otherwise experiment. Besides perfecting your persuasive angles, these other variations can also develop your speaking voice in general. I have already recommended recording, reviewing, revising, and re-recording as a method of perfecting your voice anyway. Hence, making video or audio content is a great way to get double duty out of that practice. Talk to anyone with a velvety smooth, lyrical, or otherwise unusually pleasant normal speaking voice long enough, and you will probably find a background in broadcast, public speaking, choir, or similar.

Conclusion

I hope what you have learned will be helpful to you, and the skills I have outlined and the exercises suggested will be put to good use. At this point, I will not belabor the futility of using these lessons selfishly or against the best interests of those around you any longer. The Leaning Tower of Pisa tilts because it was built on sand, and anything less than the truth is just not solid. When the time comes to apply your powers of persuasion upon your fellow humans, you should have everything you need to state your position as effectively as possible and, hopefully, pull some people around to your point of view.

Above all, remember that confidence is viewed as competency, so you had better make sure you know what you are talking about once you get going. Not only will your study and research make sure your position is well informed, but you will meet anyone assailing your perspective with detailed knowledge of all countervailing opinions. The practice you do beforehand makes sure you're not stumbling over your words and can carry forth confidently. Of course, you can fake confidence, and rehearsal will make this a flawless facade, but nothing beats genuine self-assurance.

In the information age, sniffing out lies is lies, and misinformation is becoming a crucial survival trait. You don't want to be caught on the wrong side of the truth when the situation comes to a head. No matter how clever or well-thought-out a ruse might be, the truth has a funny way of asserting itself. But there are those admonishments to be righteous again; separating fact from what is false is something of a preoccupation, and I hope you have benefited from.

It has been my pleasure to give you aid in changing minds and influencing people. With a bit of practice and a lot of awareness, there is no limit to how far a little conversational pressure can take you.

More by Lawrence Finnegan

Discover all books from the Communication Skills Series by Lawrence Finnegan at:

bit.ly/lawrence-finnegan

Book 1: Body Language

Book 2: Assertiveness

Book 3: Conversation Skills

Book 4: Persuasion

Book 5: Make People Laugh

Book 6: Small Talk

Book 7: Social Skills

Book 8: Email Etiquette

Themed book bundles available at discounted prices:

bit.ly/lawrence-finnegan

Printed in the USA
CPSIA information can be obtained
at www.ICGtesting.com
CBHW051323211024
16183CB00030B/321